TOWARDS MANAGEMENT EXCELLENCE

TOWARDS MANAGEMENT EXCELLENCE

A paradigm shift in the focus of the organization's management

SATISHKUMAR

PARTRIDGE

ISBN: Hardcover   978-1-4828-8386-2
             Softcover   978-1-4828-8387-9
             eBook   978-1-4828-8385-5

Print information available on the last page.

To order additional copies of this book, contact
Partridge India
000 800 10062 62
orders.india@partridgepublishing.com

www.partridgepublishing.com/india

CONTENTS

Preface ix

Chapter 1   Introduction to Material Resources... 1

Chapter 2   Material Resource Deployment...16

Chapter 3   MRD In Action - The Intangible Group 31

Chapter 4   The MRD Head..51

Chapter 5   MRD In Action - The Tangible Group..................................61

Chapter 6   Supplier & Customer Relationship Management..................91

Chapter 7   Concluding The MRD Concept.. 116

This book is dedicated to my wife, Jyoti, and my twin daughters, Ananya and Atulya, who encouraged and supported me to put this concept in print and to my late parents for inculcating in me the value of education.

-Satishkumar

PREFACE

Business thrives on profit. The business landscape has evolved over the years to the present day modern services as well as trade and manufacturing activities by adapting itself to the various challenges of the market and maintaining growth, profit and business continuity. Over the years, business has grown in volume, variety of business activity, and technological innovation. Ready or not, the planet is shrinking more every year and business has gone global today.

Business management, the backbone of any business, has also come a long way, ranging from the days of early business management theory by Henry Fayol in 1916 to the modern business management concepts of Peter Drucker and others during the twentieth century.

Today's business management challenges are different from those faced in earlier centuries. Business management has also evolved to meet these challenges in containing the huge growth of business in terms of volume and value, technological innovation, and a vast variety of products. As a result of globalization, business organizations are required to manage a large number of suppliers, customers, employees, as well as manage multiple manufacturing locations within and across national boundaries. *Of late, dwindling natural resources and critical environment issues have added to the business management challenges.*

The recent global economic recession collapsed entire economies in 2008. It has been considered by some as the worst crash since the great depression in the 1930s. This poses the latest challenge to business and business management. The recession has affected countries all over the world including the U.S., Japan and Germany, some of the world's largest economies. Even years later, the revival of worldwide business continues to be a challenge and is of primary concern to governments, economists, businessmen, finance and management experts all over the world. They are doing everything possible to revive dying economies.

As the world recovers from this unprecedented recession, one thing becomes clear, and that is, remaining in business and remaining profitable is going to be ever tougher. The time has come to look, think, and do differently. As Albert Einstein said, "The significant problems we face cannot be solved at the same level of thinking we were at when we created them." Therefore, the business world must now focus on innovating its business processes and look at different and better ways to remain in business and make steady profit.

In order to meet the current business challenges, this book suggests a business management innovation concept. This concept requires a paradigm shift in the focus of the organization's management from finance, marketing, or manufacturing to the material resources of the organization.

The material resources referred to here are not just the input materials for production in the case of manufacturing or goods and finished products in the case of a trading business. It also includes the finished products, the plant, and the machinery. The concept suggests looking at the entire material resources of an organization, its procurement, maintenance, its usage, re-use and finally its disposal through a focus on what I call a materials resources deployment plan. This focus will aid in the optimum use of the resources and reduce wastage, thus resulting in consistent added profit. It does not mean that we remove our focus from marketing, finance, or other business functions. On the contrary, through this concept of focus on material resources, it enhances manufacturing, supports marketing, builds supplier relationships and customer relationships and helps finance to achieve more return on its investments.

This innovation in the business process through focus on materials resources deployment of an organization is called Materials Resources Deployment – MRD, in short.

The concept places marketing, finance and HRD, as virtual owners of the organization. It dissolves the various supply chain functions within the organization and integrates them into one function, the MRD department. This improves supply chain management, helps avoid and save costs, develops a more cohesive and efficient business process, makes supplier and customer relationships extended arms of the organization's business process, and helps integrate these into the organization business process.

The MRD focus aids in homing in on material resources in terms of planning, design, procurement, transportation, usage, waste management and the avoidance of environmental pollution. This is done through re-aligning the business functions within the organization to focus on the materials resource department and its deployment, making your organization a **materials-resource-focused organization** or an **MRD organization.**

-N. SATISHKUMAR

CHAPTER 1

Introduction to Material Resources

I HAVE LABORED in the field of supply management for more than 25 years. I had the good fortune, like other business professionals of my generation, to witness during this time the enormous growth in global business and the technological innovation in every industry.

During this time we also saw the emergence of new industries such as information technology and bio-technology. The electronic products' technological revolution made computers affordable and customer friendly, the internet and cell phones revolutionized information and communication, and various business management philosophies such as TQM powered Japan into the top level in the electronics and automobile industry. This was also achieved through best practices in management such as six-sigma and others.

At a global level, business globalization and the tremendous economic growth of developing countries such as China, India and Brazil have transformed business equations drastically. The USA and the European Union, world economic powers, are presently in economic crisis and are working hard toward recovery.

I am also fortunate, not only to have witnessed the growth in the materials management field consisting of procurement, warehousing and logistics, but also to work practically with other developments that have taken place in this field over the years. All aspects of the business growth, technological development and global economy mentioned above have had a direct or indirect impact on the growth and development of the materials management function and its importance in an organization.

Thanks to TQM and the success achieved by the Japanese industry, other businesses realized the crucial importance of the suppliers in the supply chains. This made the business world aware of the potential of procurement functions and their importance to an organization. Procurement's ability to influence material quality, delivery and price highly impacts an organization's competitiveness. By proactively handling the organization's suppliers, who are today considered as partners in business, procurement has helped in strengthening the supply chain. It is because of the increased functionalities and responsibilities of procurement that it is now referred to as *supply management.*

Warehousing and logistics, two other aspects of materials management, have grown to become an essential part of the supply chain management and have also grown into niche businesses in their own right. They are popularly known as 'supply chain solutions' businesses that help you to handle all your material movements and storage requirements within your region or across the globe.

Let us now delve briefly into the importance of the materials management for an organization on a very simple level.

SUPPLY MANAGEMENT

The marketing and sales department in an organization is involved in getting orders from their customers and servicing them with the supply of products. The manufacturing department is involved in producing the required products for the organization's sale. Similarly, the materials department is involved in the procurement of materials, storing and issuing them as required by manufacturing to produce the products required by marketing and sales for their customers.

The procurement department within the materials department procures the required materials which are stored in the warehouses to maintain adequate stocks. This is known as inventory control. The materials are transported into the warehouse from suppliers locally or internationally. This is known as in-bound logistics. Warehouse issues the materials in stock to manufacturing, as required by them. After manufacturing, the shipping out of the finished products to the customers is called out-bound logistics.

Not all organizations have these three functions under one head. They may have procurement, warehousing and logistics as three different independent functions. Each function is a specialist function as they involve costs and they account for about 70 to 75% of the organization's expenses. The procurement cost is the direct cost of the materials used in a product. Warehousing accounts for storage and inventory-carrying costs, and logistics accounts for the transportation costs of the materials into the organization from the suppliers and out of the organization to the customers.

Procurement is a specialist function, as this department may well be involved in spending almost 70% of the organization's money in terms of procurement of input materials for the organization's products and services. Worldwide, therefore, professionally managed organizations entrust this function to only qualified professionals in the field of procurement, supply management or materials management. The qualified professionals in this field help the organization in professional buying by identifying qualified vendors and ensuring optimum price for the right quality material and continuity in supplies.

In a seller's market, an organization may get away with finagling input materials at very competitive prices, but the same will not be true for an organization in a buyer's market where input material costs must meet competition. This calls for professional buying and professional buyers are involved, day in and day out, working through ways and means to save costs and add to the cost savings of the organization. These savings directly contribute to the profit margin of the organization.

The importance of the procurement function has grown over the years at a national and international level. Today, the governments of many developed countries refer to the purchasing manager Index, also referred to as PMI, for gauging the economic health of their country's manufacturing and non-manufacturing sectors.

In the USA, the Institute of Supply Management (ISM), releases the PMI at the beginning of every month. This is considered as the base by which the United States government and economists relate to the economic activity of the manufacturing and non-manufacturing sectors of their nation. This is widely followed by other countries as the USA is the largest economy in the world and whatever business or economic trends are evident in the U.S. economy affect the rest of the world economies. Amongst other major countries that use the purchasing index are Germany, Japan and China. China now represents the second largest economy in the world, having replaced Japan recently in this position.

Tremendous growth in Warehousing and Logistics

The other two materials activities, warehousing and logistics, have grown from individual organizational material-related activities, to individual businesses by themselves! Businessmen have seized the opportunity of global trade and the mammoth increase in world trade over the last two decades to make forays into this business opportunity. The warehousing and logistics business has seen tremendous growth in the pioneer organizations in this business and brought in many new entrants into the field which, as mentioned earlier, is more commonly known as supply chain solutions.

World trade, which is in the trillions of dollars, consists of materials either in raw, semi or finished product form, entirely stored and moved by warehousing and transportation – big business! There is one thing common in procurement, warehousing and logistics and that is, they all deal with materials required for all types of businesses in any form. The importance of these three business activities can be understood by the fact that, the global manufacturing business volume is in fact a reflection of the material function activities of procurement, warehousing and logistics. In other words for all materials there are buyers, storage facilities and distribution through transportation. Therefore, materials in any form, are critical to any business.

IMPORTANCE OF MATERIALS TO SALES RATIO:

We have seen now how materials management and materials play a very important role in business as they physically make materials available for manufacturing and delivery of the products to the customer. 1) This activity involves cost, 2) this cost determines the selling price, 3) this selling price determines the competitiveness of the organization in the marketplace and 4) this competitiveness determines the survival of the organization and the perpetuity of the organization. When we see organizations mentioning their years of existence beside their name, it means that they are reflecting on their ability to survive by remaining competitive in the market in the long term.

A product's competitiveness is based on two aspects: one is the technology and the second is the price. A good product is one which is competitive in both. While technology determines the input materials required, the price of the input materials determines the selling price and the profit margin. As mentioned earlier, the input materials account for, in general, about 70% of the selling price of the product. It may vary based on an input material's cost and the selling price. The ratio, between the material cost and the selling price is called materials to sales ratio. This ratio is important because the lower the ratio of the material cost to the selling price the greater will be the profit to the organization.

Let me elaborate this further to establish the importance of material cost within a product's selling price-and-profit point of view.

COMPONENTS OF COST

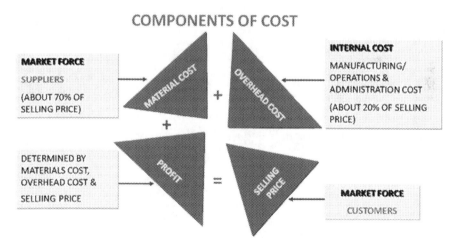

MATERIAL COST ACCOUNTS FOR ABOUT 70% OF SELLING PRICE

Let's consider the product of an organization, the sale price of which is $100 dollars. The breakdown of this price is: input materials cost of the product $70, overhead cost $20 and profit $10 (70+20+10 = 100).

The materials cost content in a product's selling price when expressed as a ratio to the selling price is called the materials to sales ratio. In the above case, the material cost is $70 and the selling price is $ 100 therefore the MS Ratio is:

materials cost x 100 =
sales price $70 x 100= 70%
$100

In the above example, the materials to sales ratio, MS ratio is 70:30

Now, in the above example, if the material cost of the product comes down by one dollar i.e. from $70 to $69 this $1 adds directly to the profit, thereby increasing profit from $10 to $11 i.e. (69+20 +11=100). This means, profit has increased by 10%.

To gain the same 10% increase in profit through the sales price will require increasing the selling price of the product by 10%. This is usually considered impossible for any company, either in a buyer's or seller's market.

There is one more way of increasing profit to the same level and that is by maintaining the same price but increasing the sales volume several fold to achieve the target profit. This is also considered very unlikely, as your volume of production is determined by your market conditions and by your capacity to put in the investment that will be required to increase production to that level.

Therefore, without increasing your selling price or increasing the volume of production you can achieve increase in profit only if you can reduce your input material's cost. In other words, you must focus on lower materials to sales ratio. This is done by procurement.

The procurement department, by developing select vendors and negotiating the best and lowest price, endeavors to achieve the lowest input costs for their organization. For any organization, this is the starting point, as the input materials and their related costs is what determines their selling price. Not all organizations can dictate their market selling price; they have to fall in line with the market price to be in business. Therefore, the importance of the procurement function becomes much greater from any organization's point of view.

Having seen the importance of material and material cost as a lifeline for an organization, an industry and the business world, let us now move onto a macro level and widen our horizons to look at the material resources from an organizational, societal, national and international point of view.

MATERIAL RESOURCES USAGE FROM A GLOBAL ANGLE:

So far, we have looked at the importance of materials management in terms of materials, its procurement cost, warehousing and transportation. Our focus was on the materials aspect related to organizations in general. Now, let us widen our horizons to a macro level and look at the same from an industrial, national, and international angle.

Business has grown tremendously worldwide over the last two decades and, with it, so has the consumption of materials. Increased manufacturing activity, mindless of environmental degradation, has led to severe eco-system problems.

While the business world's main task is to ensure business sustenance, we must look at these two vital problems the world is facing today and that is – the dwindling natural material resources and environmental pollution, both contributed undeniably by the business world.

Mahatma Gandhi said, *"Earth provides enough to satisfy everyone's need, but not everyone's greed."* In our greed to make more and more money, we in the business world, have paid little heed to the loss we were creating by mindlessly extracting the natural resources and recklessly producing without any concern for the environment and the harm being done to it.

"The world we all share is given to us in trust. Every choice we make regarding the earth, air and water around us must be with the objective of preserving it for all generations to come." We have to, therefore, take upon ourselves now the responsibility of correcting this situation to whatever extent possible. We must continue to find ways and means to preserve our natural resources for the present and, in generations to come, to find ways and means to develop alternate renewable resources. At the same time, we must find solutions to all

the environmental pollution caused at source during the extraction of material resources, the conversion process, usage and wastage and we must use the correct waste disposal methods so as not to cause harm to the environment.

I cannot refrain from quoting a very wise saying from the Art of Living founder and well known Indian spiritual guru, Sri Sri Ravi Shankar, who states: *"Half our health we spend in gaining our wealth and we spend half that wealth trying to gain back our health"*

This is very true in our business world, too. We grew the global business mindlessly to earn the billions and seriously harmed our environment in the process. We are now spending billions to rectify the wrong done to the environment! However, impacts such as climate change may be irreversible. This is frightening.

MATERIAL RESOURCES FROM A BUSINESS ANGLE:

The business world is heavily dependent upon the natural material resources for its manufacturing activities directly or indirectly. It's well known to all of us that our natural resource reserves such as coal, fossil fuels (petroleum and gas) and mineral resources (iron, aluminum, tin, carbon, silicon, zinc and copper) are fast being depleted. All these minerals are essential for our business activities and, unfortunately, they are non-renewable. We will run out of these minerals over a period of time. We may also soon be staring at fresh water shortages.

Therefore, the need of the hour is for us to make the most judicious use of the natural, material resources. We can do this by avoiding waste through mindless mining, by having a focused as well as planned usage of our material resources, and by making use of technology that will reduce the consumption of the resources, thereby increasing the reserves for the foreseeable future. Thus, a projected reserve of a natural resource for thirty years can be extended to say, forty years or more, giving us time to find alternatives and conserving this reserve further. Therefore, we must focus on the material resources.

It is also imperative on the part of our business world to use these resources in a way that during its extraction, conversion, manufacturing, transportation, usage and disposal, we do not pollute the environment. This can only happen when we modify our current technologies or invent new technologies that are used in the conversion of material resources from one form to another so that we stop polluting the environment. We must, therefore, focus on the designing of the technologies themselves which will make best use of the natural resources. Besides the two major issues of depleting natural resources and environmental degradation, the business world is faced with the challenge of reducing costs to become competitive and remain in business. Nobody will deny the fact that only a lowered, affordable price of product will see the revival of the present day recessionary market, thus enabling all of us to stay in business.

This can come through reduction in the input materials procurement cost, which helps earn more profit or a lower sales price to get more business and the proper utilization of all the material resources in the organization through proper planning, procurement, usage, maintenance and disposal using an efficient business process.

This brings us to an important aspect, which is the focus of this book, and that is the efficiency in the use of material resources by an organization in terms of:

a) Natural resource conservation by using efficient technology and avoiding waste b) Avoiding/minimizing impact on the environment as a consequence of the organization's materials use and conversion activities c) A business process that will help the organization to focus on its material resources in totality.

We will now define the material resource of an organization in the above context, as well as to meet the above-mentioned goals, enabling us to focus on the material resources.

We can say that all resources in material form used by an organization in a business should be considered as a material resource.

Therefore, in the case of a manufacturing plant, the material resources will include not only the in-put materials for its product in terms of raw materials, components, packaging materials, MROs, etc. but also the plant buildings, furniture, vehicles, equipment, machinery, tools, machinery spares, office supplies, fuel, and the finished products (a resource in material form which enables you to do business). These are all material resources for the manufacturing unit, trading or service business in the case of a material resource utility.

In case of a trading business, the office building with furniture, office supplies, vehicles, fuel, warehousing, and all the traded products that are stored in the warehouse form their material resources.

In case of a service business, the building or office facility used by the service provider, the furniture, office supplies and related equipment or instruments, vehicles, etc. form their material resources.

Having defined the material resources for the purpose of explaining the theme of this book, the MRD concept, I would like to stress a very important fact. Just as having the right technologies for manufacturing is key to avoiding poor productivity, poor quality, wastage and pollution, similarly the proper design/specifications when acquiring or building of the office premises, buildings, plants or machinery has great impact upon the efficiency of the business.

Huge amounts of money can be saved through the proper maintenance of the plant, buildings and machinery, through proper environmental- friendly architecture, civil engineering and interior design, and the use, re-use and proper disposal of office materials and equipment. Thus, using and saving energy are aspects of material resources that encompass the business as a whole. This is equally true for any type of business be it manufacturing, trading or services businesses.

Let me explain this further.

Take the example of a manufacturing unit. Let us assume it does not plan and design its office building and plant in the proper way. It does not buy/use the best technology for manufacturing and does not design and develop the right materials and specification of the input materials.

The impact of these factors in the long term will result in inadequate space for employees in the office building as the business grows and not enough space for machine and process layout and material movement across the shop floor. Inadequate technology will result in sub-standard products that will not match the competition and in improper technology which could add to wastage and pollution in the process of manufacturing. The incorrectly designed or engineered input materials will lead to higher cost if over-designed and poor quality products if under-designed, making the final product not able to rise above the competition in the market.

Similarly, in case of a trading business, it has to pay close attention in the designing of its office building, as mentioned above, and ensure that its warehouses are designed to carry enough inventory to meet the growing business demand. It must ensure proper storage system, enough space for material movement and use of the right material-handling equipment to avoid any accidents. It must also look into the fleet efficiency for delivery of its products to customers by having the right type of vehicles, well maintained so as to control pollution as well as being fuel efficient.

In case of a service business, the most important aspect of materials resource is their office or buildings. For example, in the case of a consultant, it will be reflected in how well he designs his office to meet requirements in terms of work environment as well as aesthetics to impress his clients. For a hospital, the space, ventilation and the quality of the various rooms as well as critical or non-critical instruments and equipment used for the patients' treatment will form the main material resources for such a service industry.

Therefore, you will note that whether for a business organization, a manufacturing unit, a trading business, or a service-oriented business, the facility or production requirements are all materials based. **This leads us to one important fact: any type of business is in some way material-resource oriented.**

We have the ability to control these material resources at the time of inception, during use, and at the time of disposal. It all depends upon how each business unit focuses on the material resources to make it competitive through right planning, design, usage and maintenance of all material resources related to its business. Any inadequacies will lead to costs directly or indirectly—that is business losses which may or may not be evident initially.

Having seen that every business is materials-resource oriented, let us now look at various industries in regard to how they are interrelated. This will furnish us with a comprehensive view of the material resource utilization.

INTERLINK OF MATERIAL RESOURCES

All industries in business are interlinked directly or indirectly through the material resources as the finished product of one becomes the input for the other and, therefore, makes them dependent on each other for operations.

Let's take the example of a plastic molder.

A plastic molder is engaged in the manufacture of various plastic parts or components at a molding facility. The owner uses plastic extrusion machines to extrude plastic components out of resins. Now, the molding machine in his plant is the product of another manufacturer who makes machines and the input material resin comes from the resin manufacturer. His plant and office building facilities are constructed by a construction company whose product is any civil construction or civil works.

We can note that the output of one business unit is the input for another business unit. Therefore, all businesses are connected with each other directly or indirectly. This means that all existing businesses are interconnected with providing material resources for some business or the other.

The material resources, therefore, interlink businesses and become an important factor in working with each other to focus on prudent consumption, protection of the environment, and reduction in costs. One organization by itself cannot work on all of these facets. It requires input agencies such as materials and technology suppliers to provide input that can meet this end and it, in turn, ensures that it gives to its customers the same. *This will create the link between one producer and the eventual consumer and set a chain reaction to achieve material or energy consumption reduction, avoid pollution of the environment, and enable overall efficiency.*

EVERY PRODUCT IS 100% MATERIAL Now, let us look also at a finished product which is 100% material.

In terms of cost, all material-based products carry an average of 70% of material cost in their price. The other 30% is contributed through process cost, overhead, and profit. This, as mentioned earlier, is called the MS ratio i.e. materials to sales ratio. A lower or higher material content percentage is dependent on the price of a product, which is determined by the demand for the product and a market that allows for higher pricing or lower pricing.

Therefore, is it obvious that, with material resources constituting such a large percentage of business unit, we must focus on better management of the material resource.

This focus will help us:

a) To plan and design excellent facilities and input materials and manufacturing processes that conserve material, are energy efficient, and do not pollute the environment. Reduce waste at every stage from material extraction, conversion, storage, and transportation—right up to final consumption.
b) Plan re-use and/or disposal of waste in a manner that will not harm the environment.
c) Reduction of unnecessary costs and inefficiency, resulting in cost savings.

In order to meet the above, we will require more efficient business and manufacturing processes.

Therefore, the time has come to focus on the materials aspect of business. This means that the business world must now make a paradigm shift in its focus on business management from a market/finance oriented focus to a materials resource focused management. In other words, business must now focus on the material content of their products and a plant must hone in on its usage, that is, to cut waste, reduce usage, control/use non-polluting processes to protect environment and reduce costs through judicious materials resource management. *This means that all those in the business world must now become material-resource and environmentally conscious citizens.*

We will now see how we can move toward meeting this goal.

TOWARDS MATERIAL RESOURCE DEPLOYMENT:

In business, we have seen over the years many concepts that have worked toward waste elimination, productivity efficiency, quality improvement and cost reduction. Processes which have proved effective include re-engineering, single-piece-flow, value engineering, value analysis and 6-sigma techniques.

Various well known heads of multi-national organizations have contributed their own personal styles and initiatives to turn around loss making corporations into profit-making units and helped organizations to retain their leadership in the market. Their success stories have been studied and have benefited the business world as a whole.

Similarly, we also have the Supply Chain Management (SCM), a business model that has benefited businesses. SCM links certain aligned business activities within an organization such as marketing, materials, manufacturing and logistics to improve their coordination and ensure smooth flow of materials in various stages before, during, and after manufacturing. It then links the suppliers to the organization to form the upstream activity and the customers as the downstream activity to complete the supply chain.

The Supply Chain Management coordinates the flow of materials into a manufacturing or trading organization from the suppliers. After the material is received, the organization carries out necessary conversion processes (re-packing, if required, in case of a trading unit) and it transports and delivers the final product to the customer.

Unfortunately, supply chain management suffers from a major problem and that is – it is only a model within the business unit that aligns these activities.

Individuals from the aligned activities such as marketing, procurement, manufacturing and logistics must somehow coordinate with each other. However, the responsibilities of the individual department that come under this model are not under one head. Each function such as manufacturing, engineering, procurement, quality or logistics is a different department under its respective leader.

Therefore, even if the responsibility of supply chain is entrusted to one head, he has no direct leverage, control, or influence over the various departments in the supply chain. The supply chain "leader" cannot direct manufacturing, engineering, procurement or other departments that link the supply chain.

This effectively disables the supply chain coordinator from having authority in the supply chain to direct, control or make decisions as required to meet the desired goals or targets of the supply chain.

In order to benefit from the SCM model, we need to now move on to the next step of SCM evolvement that will enable consolidation of SCM activities under one head within the organization.

This is possible through a focus on all the material resources of the organization by bringing these resources under the control of one head who will be responsible for the management and deployment of the organization's material resources.

How this can occur efficiently and smoothly I will explain to you in the next chapter.

CHAPTER 2

Material Resource Deployment

IN ANY MANUFACTURING unit there are various business activities that work independently as well as in coordination with other functions in the organization.

For example, marketing finds their customer independently but coordinates with design or engineering departments for the technical specifications of the product being offered to the customer and relies on manufacturing for delivery of the products ordered by the customer.

The technical department, design or engineering, designs the product but relies on purchasing for ensuring the availability in the market of the materials they specify. They also ensure that the manufacturing department has the capability to produce as per the specifications of the product.

In this manner, all departments in the organization carry out various functions independently as they also rely on other departments to give the right input for fulfilling their role. However, the prime responsibility lies with the department concerned and in the event of lack of coordination, cooperation, a communication gap or any misunderstanding, the department concerned gets the blame. It is at this point that often the 'finger-pointing' and 'passing-the-buck' game starts.

In case of a major mess-up, the organization's internal meetings look like a battle scene with tempers flaring and allegations, counter-allegations, proofs and evidences flying across the meeting room! One of the euphemisms for 'I am preparing for a meeting' is 'I am arming myself to attack others and protect myself in whatever manner possible'!

While the above may or may not be true for every organization, you will definitely agree that a similar situation often takes place in the intra-organization e-mails!

Well, at the end of the day everyone wants to protect their own job and therefore, be it marketing, manufacturing, procurement or any other department, they at least attempt to fulfill their respective roles and coordinate with other departments to the extent possible to ensure the completion of business activities within the organization. *It is the efficiency of this business process within the organization that determines the success of the organization in fulfilling customer orders on time and with fine quality.*

DRAWBACK IN THE PRESENT ORGANIZATIONAL SYSTEM

While some of our organizations stumble along in this manner and survive, we face a major problem. The problem is that the present system makes our employees in various departments work in watertight compartments. We work for the department we are in and ensure that we do our part of the work in contribution to the company's goal but we leave the rest strictly to the others.

In other words, it is somewhat like the 400 meter relay. Each runner runs their lap the best he or she can, then hands over the baton to the other. This is fine in a business until the inter-related functions come to light. That's the time when coordination, cooperation and combined teamwork between two or more business functions are required and this is what makes the difference between *efficiency* and *effectivity*.

Each department feels that they have done their job, but business management is not about any function working on its own. There is a 20% or 30% definite direct or indirect overlap between all the functions in an organization. This is the point where coordination, cooperation, communication, knowledge and experience come into play. This point tests our truthfulness, wisdom and integrity. Many a time, this point also becomes a major decision making moment. When this overlap aspect is missed between two, three, four or more departments, a major mishap or mistake in the business process occurs. The blame is not on the individuals concerned but the faulty system. This is the problem we all face in our organizations - inter-department and interrelated functions require coordination.

TQM offered a solution to this problem through the internal customer concept whereby the dependent function becomes the customer of the function it is dependent upon. Therefore, if marketing is dependent on manufacturing to service its customers with the ordered products, marketing becomes the internal customer of manufacturing. Be it internal or external customer (the actual customers) the aim of TQM was 'Customer satisfaction.'

TQM rectified the inter-department problem to a certain extent through the internal customer service and satisfaction concept. However, although it's a good business practice, there was no binding compulsion for any department to meet the internal customer requirements. What is required and is missing is a combination of all the related activities under one head so that there is no differentiation of departments under various heads.

Individual departments may function okay with their respective heads, but the company may not be reaching near peak efficiency. However, if all the allied business activities were brought under one head, the company should function better!

Imagine the difference when the allied activities like manufacturing, materials, engineering and quality control are brought under one head. The entire activities of these three functions will be well coordinated and the result will be far better than when they function individually.

This combination, merging related activities under one head, will look like a sports team, say, a football team. The 'business team' must work like the football team that has players of various roles, each one playing their role at their best and also combining as a team to put in their best effort under one captain. Our organizations can also work in this manner.

Allow me to expand on this thought to imagine some further improvement on the team aspect and team work. How would it be if the football team has players who are well-rounded i.e. each player could play in any position? The captain would be the happiest person. He could use any player anywhere during the play, be it as a forward or back, and maneuver his players as the situation of an ongoing game demands. So, too, in a business team, the business captain can shuffle his "players" i.e. his professionals on his team for any assignment as the situation demands.

Thus, it is advantageous if business can be viewed from this perspective and you will see as I take you through to the MRD concept that follows shortly.

SHORTCOMING OF THE SUPPLY CHAIN MANAGEMENT

Supply Chain Management (SCM) interlinks various business activities within and without the organization in a chain of interrelated business functions or activities. This enables better tracking and flow of materials right from the supplier through to the organization activities and right up to the customer. However, as mentioned earlier, the main problem with SCM is that it is only a model within an organization. Even if a team with a head is assigned to handle the supply chain management of the organization, they do not have any direct control or say in the various departments that handle the organization's business activities. They face the following problems:

1) SCM team has no control in the manufacturing or engineering activities on a day-to-day basis.
2) Even if the SCM team has representatives from the allied activities from various departments, the team members report functionally and administratively to their respective department heads instead of a centralized leadership.

This results in limitations upon the SCM team to perform.

In other words, with the SCM shortcoming mentioned above, we are still at the 400 meter relay performance level in our organization's business activity. Therefore, it is obvious now that we should bring all the related business activities under one head.

Thus there is a crucial need to have a paradigm shift in our present way of looking at our organizational structure from a business-activity based to materials-resource based business organization structure.

HOW CAN WE CREATE A MATERIALS RESOURCE BASED ORGANIZATION STRUCTURE?

Let us take the example of a medium scale manufacturing unit.

It consists of plant, warehouse, machinery, equipment, tools, spare parts, administration office buildings, office equipment and furniture, raw materials and components and finished products. As defined earlier, all these fall under the material category and, as such, become the materials resource of the business unit.

After establishing the material base of the manufacturing unit, let us now look at the various business activities within the manufacturing unit that deal directly with material.

You will note that manufacturing, purchasing, warehousing, engineering and sales handle the material directly in some form or the other. Whereas marketing, finance and HRD do not directly deal with materials.

Therefore, we can conclude that in an organization, the business materials-based and material-related business activities form a major value in the business unit. Therefore, even a 1% improvement in the efficiency of the material-based resources or material-related business activities is direct profit. The logical question that now comes to mind from a business management point of view is:

Can the entire materials-based resources and material-related business activities be brought under one head so that the materials resource and business activity is **focused** for better management and deployment.

Yes, this is possible. We will do so through *the **MRD** concept. **This will require you to re-vamp our organizational structure to focus on the material resources of your organization.***

PARADIGM SHIFT AND THE POWER OF FOCUS

In order to achieve our goal of focusing on materials resources, we must take the bold step of reorganizing our present set-up within the organization. Hence, we need to have a paradigm shift in our present focus from marketing, manufacturing or finance to material resources. This paradigm shift does not mean that we lose focus on the other business functions. On the other hand, a focus on the material resources will result in better performance of the other business functions. And the new organizational set-up, as you will see shortly, will free the CEO to focus more on marketing and finance!

Now, let us dwell a little on the power of focus.

Friends, whatever we focus on in life, that is directing our full attention, effort, and energy toward the thing, this is the job which gets done. If you are exercising control on something and you focus your attention on it, that thing remains under a state of control as we desire.

For example, if you focus on achieving a business management degree, you will automatically spend lesser time and attention on other things to find time to attend to your studies and achieve your goal. Since the 9/11 attack by terrorists on the World Trade Centre, the American government has realigned its various agencies and focused on internal security. A decade later, the effectiveness of this focus by the concerned top authorities is obviously evident - no significant untoward incidents have occurred since then. That's the power of focus.

At international and national levels also, when there is a natural calamity, citizens, the media, governments and NGOs all focus their attention and resources to help to resolve the crisis. This focus helps in getting all necessary aid to the needy faster.

When heads of governments, organizations or institutions focus on resolving matters of importance or concern, things happen. A recent example is the BP oil spill in the Gulf of Mexico in 2010. The U.S. president, Barack Obama, took the initiative to personally get involved and review the problem, visit the site, launch the government machineries and BP into action to contain the spill. That's the power of focus.

This reminds me of the Indian Bhopal Gas tragedy in the year 1984 when the dangerous methyl isocyanine leak took place from the Union Carbide gas plant, killing thousands of people. Even after more than twenty-five years, 350 metric tonnes of toxic waste lying at the site, is yet to be disposed. That's the power of non-focus by the concerned authorities!

Yet, one more example that comes to mind is about the power of focus on negative subjects. We have seen over the years, English movies basing their stories on violence – machine guns, bombs and killings. This negative focus may well have inspired terrorists to convert those films into reality!

In business, too, all over the planet, most CEOs of business organizations focus first and foremost on marketing and finance. The reason is that, without sales orders and money flow, an organization cannot survive. And what does that focus result in? It ensures that the CEOs remain focused on the healthy condition of the organization in terms of booked orders and sound financial position. This focus also helps the CEOs to catch the first signals of any business problems or expected problems so that these can be dealt with well preemptively.

Similarly, if we were to direct the power of our *focus on materials resources*, hitherto ignored, we would reap the profits thereof. After all, a materials resource, as seen earlier, forms a very major constituent of our business. Allow me to illustrate.

FOCUS ON MATERIAL RESOURCES

A manufacturing plant with its facilities, buildings, machinery and equipment are 100% material resources.

Any product is 100% material and the selling price consists of, on an average, 70% materials cost. In other words, a company with one billion dollars worth of sales uses about 700 million dollars worth of materials. Add to this the inventory of materials in the warehouse waiting to be used, finished products waiting in the finished goods warehouses for shipping, and materials in transit headed for the organization's warehouse.

Is it not obvious that the handling of materials is absolutely crucial to the bottom line expenditures and profits? In view of its high value, definitely the power of focus must be here and, if done with an intention for optimum utilization, it can result in huge savings for the organization.

Therefore, it is prudent to direct our FOCUS on the entire materials resource of an organization by bringing the materials resources under one head. This will focus on avoiding waste and ensuring efficient utilization of all resources to gain maximum benefit. If we produce even 1% saving in the overall material resources costs, this is significant because it adds directly to the profit.

We discussed that procurement works on the input materials for reducing costs on a continuous basis. Regarding other material resources, maintaining efficiently a facility or organizational assets avoids or postpones maintenance/ repair expenses for the organization, which directly saves money. For example, well maintained machinery lasts longer, furnishes maximum output, saves on maintenance and down time costs and increases productivity. Well maintained buildings and facilities avoid regular civil maintenance expenses. Besides creating a positive image for the organization to clients, it creates a good environment in which employees can work and perform.

Let me interject, although it is bit of diversion from our course, the materials resource conservation can be of similar importance for a nation also. If the governments of each country were to focus on improving the utilization of their material resources, which might run into billions of dollars, even 0.5% savings would be enormous. Governments must focus on reducing wastage of material resources and the under-utilization or non-utilization of their resources. Hence, there is a need for the governments, too, to focus on their material resources and establish a material resources deployment ministry to control the government-owned resources. Good luck!

ORGANIZING THE MATERIAL RESOURCES UNDER ONE HEAD

In order to bring all material resources and direct material-related business activities under one head, to aid in our understanding we will consider an example of the outsourcing concept to achieve this end.

As mentioned earlier, the business world has seen many business improvement concepts that have genuinely benefited the bottom lines of the organizations. One such successful concept that has found great acceptance is outsourcing. Actually outsourcing is a recycled concept which was prevalent when manufacturing firms in earlier eras started farming out less critical components to outside vendors. Formerly, this was referred to as farmed-out or bought-out components.

Later on this concept caught on once again when entrepreneurs started setting up businesses such as foundry, plating, machining and fabrication set-ups that helped the manufacturing firms fulfill their requirements from such vendors. This saved the manufacturing firms investment of time, effort and manpower by avoiding such jobs themselves.

Today, manufacturing firms focus on doing only their core manufacturing activity and procuring the rest of the items and components from their vendors. Globalization has led to foreign outsourcing; and, today, sourcing from low-cost countries such as China and India has become a popular attraction to save on costs of input materials. Products created in such countries take advantage of the low wage and materials cost.

Well, China must be incredibly grateful for the outsourcing concept! In great part, China's tremendous growth has been spurred by global manufacturers outsourcing from China. This is undoubtedly due to China's highly competitive labor rates and material prices.

However, on the other hand, outsourcing has affected the U.S. economy adversely in some cases. The United States manufacturing base has been reduced drastically, thereby affecting jobs in the manufacturing industry. Personally, I feel that the USA is going through a realignment process in business such that the high level of joblessness may lead citizens to accept lower salaries. This will, in turn, help small and medium industries to start up again and jobs can be created. The United States government must also aid such entrepreneurs to establish low investment cost industries, subsidize materials in terms of tax exemptions and entry into such specified categories should be a no, no to the multinationals or large corporations. The 'mantra' or the golden rule here is "from big to small to grow big again." The MRD concept would be one more solution for the U.S. manufacturing sector to revive!

One more area for business development for every country would be to encourage re-cycling companies by giving tax exemptions, protection, technology aid, bank loans and other business incentives. This will help new entrepreneurs in the small/medium scale sectors to enter this field and multiplied tons of materials wasted around the globe can be reused, saving our natural resources as well as creating employment.

We now look at the outsourcing concept from a different angle, and that is applying the outsourcing principal within the organization! We will call it:

INTRA-ORGANIZATION OUTSOURCING!

In order to focus on material resources, we must segregate the direct materials-related business activities from the other non-material or indirect material-related business activities.

If we look at our business activities within the organization, we will note that there are two types of activities to be segregated *as **Tangible** and **Intangible*** business activities.

Let me first explain the aspect of tangible business activities.

TANGIBLE BUSINESS ACTIVITIES

Tangible activities are those business activities that deal directly with materials or require materials to perform their function. The results of their activities can be seen in physical form through handling, moving, or conversion of the material. Therefore, such activities are called ***tangible activities.***

Thus manufacturing activities are comprised of: 1) materials being converted from raw material to final products, 2) procurement: purchasing materials and transporting them and delivering them to warehouses, 3) handling, storage and issue of materials to manufacturing by warehousing, engineering, 4) using machines, materials and equipment for manufacturing, 5) civil engineers dealing with materials for construction activities, 6) quality control or inspection departments inspecting materials or products, 7) R&D and design department developing products, 8) sales department arranging transportation and delivery of products to their customers. All these fall under the tangible business activities.

Now let us look at the intangible business activities.

INTANGIBLE BUSINESS ACTIVITIES

Intangible business activities are concerned with material resources but do not utilize them directly to perform their business activities. These are called *intangible activities.*

Let's take the example in finance. They plan, account, record, review, transact, report all in fine print in terms of data, graphics and statistics. They do this for all accounting and financial transactions. Yes, they do work with one material aspect and that is business checks, paper money and coins! This money is not usually in physical form except for the petty cash they carry on a daily basis. Their resource money is stored in the bank by the bank. We all know that not even the banks carry those millions in hard cash. It is all in the form of figures on paper. Imagine a multinational company, worth millions of dollars, holding all its cash within itself and not in a bank. It would require warehouses to store the money. Try adding the security needs to that!

Now let's look at marketing. Their activity is to develop customers and get orders. If you look at marketing, there is no material involved in their activity. The customer orders are produced by manufacturing and delivered to the customers, which actually is a role of the sales and logistics department. Here, we understand the responsibility of marketing as the department that works for market creation and acquiring orders for the organization. The sales department will be responsible for actual execution of the order in terms of delivery to the customers.

Although marketing considers it their responsibility to ensure that the customers receive their ordered materials, they are actually not handling the product. They can do without it as long as the sales department ensures that the ordered products are delivered to them on time. *This brings us to an important point:*

Marketing, therefore, is an intangible activity and sales is a tangible activity which is a material resource- based activity.

We will now consider HRD. These provide the most important and vital resource for carrying out a business activity - Human resource. Their main activities are to recruit, train, retain, promote or retrench the employees. They do not deal with any material resource directly and therefore, obviously, HRD does not qualify in the tangible category.

After this broad categorizing of **tangible** and **intangible** aspects of business activities, we can see that three business activities stand out as the **intangible** activities. They are **marketing, finance** and **HRD**. All other activities fall under the **tangible** category as they are connected with material resource activity. They are:

purchasing, manufacturing/production, operations, sales, warehousing, logistics, engineering, design, quality control/assurance, inspection, R&D, maintenance, IT, civil engineering, material handling and safety and environment (directly involved with the process and handling of all safety equipment, gadgets and environmental monitoring instruments).

In the case of the IT department, in a manufacturing unit, once the software (say an ERP) is established, they are required to work chiefly on maintenance of hardware and de-bugging any software-related issues. They deal with computers, servers and other electronic equipment related to IT and therefore their work becomes a tangible activity like mechanical, electrical, electronics, or instrumentation under engineering.

Now, between these two sets of business activities, tangible and intangible, we note that the **intangible business activities hold sway over the organizational activities** because marketing provides the orders, finance provides the money, and HRD provides the human resources. Tangible business activities are dependent on the intangible activities to carry on the manufacturing and supply products to the customers. On the other hand, the entire performance of marketing, finance and HRD is dependent on the effective use and cost effective output of the tangible group with the material resources.

Thus, we are now able to distinguish our business activities into two distinct set of activities: one that uses material resources directly and the other that provides this group with the necessary support to utilize the material resources of the organization.

A HYPOTHETICAL BUSINESS SCENE:

We will now discuss 'intra-organizational outsourcing' for which we will have to consider a hypothetical business scene.

Let us imagine that the three intangible business activities – marketing, finance and HRD get together as business partners. Marketing brings the orders, finance has the money to invest and HRD can arrange human resources for a business activity by providing talented human resources at a competitive cost.

The intangible group business partners are now ready with orders, money, and human resource. All they require is a manufacturing agent that will use the money for arranging all required materials to produce the marketing orders by utilizing the talented human factor.
Therefore, in the intra-organizational outsourcing hypothesis business case, the intangible group will now approach the tangible group within the organization that directly handles all the materials resources of the organization.

The intangible group partners, let's call them 'Intangible Material Resource Corporation (IMRC) will now contract their orders to the tangible group called 'Tangible Material Resource Corporation (TMRC) to make the products!

TMRC is expected to make the products at an agreed-upon price or even better in order to enable IMRC to rake in more profit.

With this in mind, we can consider that IMRC in the organization has outsourced their manufacturing requirements to TMRC. That's it; we have now a classic example of intra-organizational outsourcing!

We must dwell a little more on the outsourcing concept and reflect the same in our hypothetical case.

Outsourcing is done when we do not have the facility to produce or creation of the provision is costly or uneconomical. The other reason is, we can make a choice from the various available sources and go to the best in terms of quality, delivery and price. Definitely, we can change source anytime the source does not live up to these expectations. Keeping this same facet in mind, from a business angle, the IMRC group will expect the same from the TMRC group. The expectations of the three partners in the IMRC group, marketing, finance and HRD will be as follows:

Marketing will expect TMRC to manufacture the marketing customer orders at a price that will provide a good profit margin, good quality, timely delivery, good after-sales services and continuous improvement in manufacturing technology and product quality and innovation.

Finance, who provides TMRC with the money for arranging all the material resources to produce the marketing orders, will expect product sales profit and a return on investments.

HRD will expect TMRC to work with the optimum requirement of human resources so that it will not overspend the human resource budget.

THE MATERIALS RESOURCE DEPLOYMENT:

The responsibility of the tangible group towards the intangible group starts now.

To continue using our hypothetical case, with the entire tangible resource, (which we will now refer to as 'materials resources') at their disposal, TMRC is in a position to meet the requirements of IMRC. They now need to pool all their material resources, and plan, procure, produce the product, and deliver fine quality to the customers of IMRC products. TMRC's expenses should not exceed that which it has committed to IMRC. If it produces at costs under budget, it will only add more profit!

Of course, they are under the delineations of IMRC and therefore must ensure all safety and environment requirements in their conversion process, the failing of which they may bring legal action as per contract! They cannot waste material and therefore must re-cycle wherever possible, sell waste to other users or dispose waste in a manner that will not harm the environment. They must design products that will ensure conservation of energy and other utilities, input material, and continuously carry out value engineering, value analyses and reengineering activities to ensure optimum use of all material resources at their disposal i.e. materials, machinery and manufacturing facility. Besides this, they must handle the supplier and customer relationship such that this relationship becomes the extended left and right arms of the organization.

This calls for very shrewd planning, acquiring, directing, controlling and deployment for optimum utilization of all the material resources of the tangible organization. *We can call this the **Materials Resource Deployment – MRD** in short and the department that is entrusted with this activity in an organization is the* **MRD department**.

Therefore, the TMRC in our hypothetical case now becomes the MRD department in the organization and will work toward meeting the expectations of the IMRC i.e. marketing, finance and HRD. The combined performance of the IMRC and the TMRC groups culminates in the performance of the organization.

Now let us for a moment look at this concept from a philosophical angle and then from a logical business angle.

Philosophically, what we have done is a paradigm shift in our way of looking at business activities in an organization. We have brought the action-oriented group members in the organization together to play as in a football game, and have looked at the impact of FOCUS on the highest value of the physical assets of the business –the material resources.

Logically, we have now aligned all material-resources-related activities and processes together under one head for synergizing the utilization of material resources.

We will now see, in the next chapter, how the MRD concept actually works in a real organization.

CHAPTER 3

MRD In Action - The Intangible Group

IN THE PREVIOUS chapter, we defined the Materials Resource Deployment [MRD] concept through the tangible and intangible business activities within an organization.

We will now see how the MRD concept works practically in an organization.

Let us consider a medium scale manufacturing unit to understand our concept. Later on, we will see how the same concept can be applied to large scale and multinational organizations. Actually, as I see it, large organizations are, in fact, a multiplying factor of a medium scale business unit. Therefore, if we can organize a medium scale organization along the lines of the MRD concept, the same will be possible with larger organizations also. Let me explain.

We will take the example of a fan manufacturing unit which, let us say, produces about 50,000 fans per month by labor from 100 employees. Now, the demand goes up for the fans by 100% i.e. 100,000 fans per month. Therefore, the unit will add more machinery and equipment and employ more workers, say another 75 employees, not exactly double, as there will be upward gradation in technology, some automation and better productivity. This unit, with the increase in volume, is now growing into a large organization.

The demand now goes up further to 150,000 fans per month. The existing plant can no more take additional production owing to capacity limitation and space problems. Therefore, the business unit decides to set up a new plant with the latest technology and a provision to increase the capacity if more orders come in. The unit is now a large scale organization.

More luck and fortune comes to the unit as, based on its reputation as a manufacturer of quality fans, the export customers double up orders on the unit!

The business unit realizes that 40% of its production is exports and all the fans are exported to Far Eastern countries. Therefore, there is no point in manufacturing the same in Europe and sending it all the way to the Far East. Therefore, it decides to set up shop in China and cater to the market of the Far East from its new plant in China which works out far easier and cheaper!

Now our business unit, has expanded from a medium scale company into a large scale fan manufacturing company and, thereafter, by setting up a plant in China has now become a multinational company!

This is what I call the multiplying effect in the growth of an organization. In other words, it is the magnification of the activities that go on in a medium scale unit that doubles up or grows a number of times. Some organizations stay with one family of products or some diversify into various other fields of business. The underlying principle remains the same if we are talking about growth from 'small to large.' The basic fundamentals of business management remain the same but the challenge is in the management of the increasing volume in terms of input material, manufacturing capabilities, additional funds and more people.

In the above example, although the business has grown from a medium scale business to a multinational business organization, MRD will function in each unit of this organization. The MRD heads of each unit will coordinate with each other to synergize their respective best practices coordinated by the CEO.

In case of organizations having distribution warehouses at various local or international locations, the same will be handled by sales which, you will see later, will be a part of the MRD department. There is good scope for MRD to outsource this activity since, as mentioned earlier, warehousing and logistics providers are doing a great job in this field in terms of timely delivery, efficient storage and handling, and inventory control.

MRD ORGANIZATIONAL CHART

Before we put MRD concept in action, we must develop the organizational chart based on the same. This will help us understand clearly the organizational set up under the new concept. The organizational chart based on the MRD concept of a medium scale unit will be along the lines of tangible material resources and intangible material resources. We will have three business functions under the intangible material heading – marketing, finance and HRD and one function under tangible materials resources - MRD. All other tangible business activities related to materials resources will fall under MRD.

Before we make the MRD organizational chart, let us first visit our conventional organizational chart for a medium scale business unit. This is to understand the current working of the organizational structure and then compare it with the MRD organizational structure so that we can understand the difference in the MRD structure as well as enable the author to explain the new structure.

ORGANIZATIONAL CHART
OF OUR CONVENTIONAL ORGANIZATION

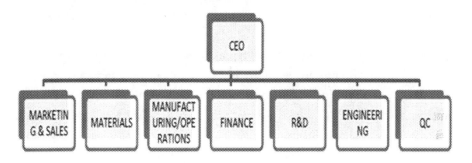

As can be seen, the medium scale business unit has a CEO to head the unit and has the following business activities or departments reporting directly to him:

Marketing, sales, finished goods warehouse & logistics, finance, materials (procurement, warehousing & logistics), manufacturing/operations, planning, engineering (maintenance), quality control, HRD, R&D, safety and environment.

In our conventional set up of a medium scale company, all the major operations report directly to the CEO. He decides on the annual budget, monthly production plan based on marketing orders, product development, customer complaints, review of quality issues, capacity enhancement and coordinates on a regular basis with the above heads of the department and occasionally has a review meeting with the respective departments.

The performance of the organization depends upon how well the various departments interact and work together. Secondly, it depends on the CEO as to how well he coordinates and directs all the departments and interacts with them on a routine basis to ensure meeting day to day, weekly and monthly objectives to achieve the annual budget targets.

The approach here for each function/department is to ensure that they complete their respective tasks (let's ensure our increments!). They are not concerned about the other departments nor do the other departments require them to get involved in their activities.

Even if a supply chain team exists, [a coordination team consisting of material, manufacturing, engineering, marketing, sales and logistics], they will be more involved in ensuring that they do their part of the task only. As mentioned earlier, the SCM team member is not reporting administratively or functionally to the SCM coordinator or leader. He has no decision-making powers nor can he influence the decisions of his head of department who will not be directly involved with SCM on a day to day activity basis. The SCM members will also have their own responsibilities to be fulfilled from a department angle and hence will not be able to dedicate enough time for the SCM activities.

Now let us look at the organizational chart based on the MRD concept.

The organizational chart for the same medium scale organization we drew above, based on our conventional structure, will look as follows in terms of the MRD concept:

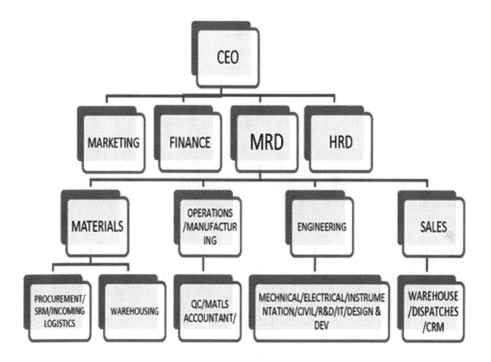

Organizational Chart under the MRD concept

The above MRD organization is based on our segregation of the material resource activities into tangible and intangible activities. Therefore, we have placed under MRD all the allied tangible activities, while the intangible activities stand separately i.e. finance, marketing and HRD.

We now have the four heads of department reporting to the CEO. This makes the CEO's job much easier. The MRD head takes care of all the manufacturing-related activities and becomes the one point of contact for the CEO. The MRD head coordinates with the marketing head directly which enables him to be in total awareness of all the marketing requirements as well as market developments. As the MRD head is now in direct control of all the resources, he will be in perfect position to maneuver all his resources to meet the marketing requirement as all the main functions of manufacturing, materials, engineering and sales are directly under his authority. In the present set-up neither manufacturing nor materials nor engineering are in full control of meeting the marketing requirement. It is the 400 meter relay in which each one runs their lap and hands over the baton to the concerned process.

THE MRD BUSINESS PROCESS:

Having drawn up the organizational chart based on MRD concept, we will now see how the business process works under this concept.

Upon formation of a MRD department, the first responsibility of this department will be to work out the pricing of all the products the organization manufactures. As you will see later, the MRD team will have a cost accountant who, along with purchasing, manufacturing and engineering (remember, they are all one team now) will work out accurate pricing of the product considering materials and process cost and the accountant will ensure the finance aspect of the pricing in terms of depreciation etc. Once all the cost aspects of the products are taken into consideration, MRD will pass it on to marketing who, along with the CEO, will decide the pricing policy of the product(s).

For standard products the price can be reviewed every month so that marketing can note any change and revise price if necessary. For pricing order to order, as in the case of tailor made or custom based products or even tenders, MRD will forward the costing to marketing on a case-to-case basis.

Marketing will forward all the customer orders and contracts to the MRD head who will review it along with his team of manufacturing, engineering, sales and logistics and cost accountants to ensure that the technical specifications, manufacturing capability and commercial terms are understood and agreeable. MRD then plans for materials and production.

Upon production, sales and logistics arrange to deliver the product to the customer. Sounds like an 'All in one' concept, doesn't it!

Yes, we have now achieved one of the paramount goals of removing the hurdle which Supply Chain Management faced within the original organization. *You will see that now the entire supply-chain related activities are under one head!*

Therefore, the SCM concept within the organization now is dissolved as all the links in the supply chain viz-a-viz materials, manufacturing, engineering, quality control, sales and logistics which required unhandy coordination and cooperation in separate departments, are now under one head. The MRD department now becomes the only link in the supply chain with the suppliers and customers forming the other part of the supply chain.

Therefore, the MRD concept now creates a new SUPPLY CHAIN MODEL and that is:

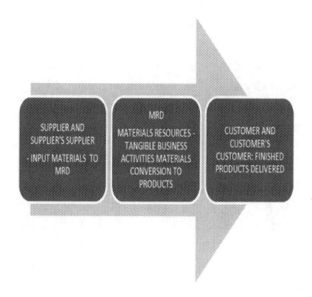

SRM MRD CRM

The Supplier Relationship Management (SRM) and the Customer Relationship Management (CRM) are most crucial for the success of any organization. This will be handled by the MRD department. We will deal with this aspect in detail in Chapter 6.

Having explained briefly above how the business model under MRD works, I will now go into an in-depth explanation of how the intangible and tangible material resources activities will work in an organization under the MRD concept.

As the MRD concept has made a paradigm shift in the organizational structure, it therefore alters some of the responsibilities carried out by various departments in our conventional organization structure.

We will start with the INTANGIBLE business activities.

INTANGIBLE BUSINESS ACTIVITIES

Let us recollect the hypothetical intra-organizational outsourcing case we discussed earlier in Chapter2.

IMRC, the Intangible Materials Resource Corporation, consisting of business partners: marketing, finance and HRD, had outsourced their manufacturing requirements to a materials resource oriented group TMRC, the Tangible Materials Resource Corporation which we now call the MRD department.

The responsibilities and roles of the two groups changed, although consisting of the same business functions we have in our conventional business model today.

We will now look at the roles and responsibilities of the intangible group i.e. marketing, finance and HRD in this chapter and the intangible group termed the MRD in Chapter 5.

MARKETING:

Under the MRD concept, in our paradigm shift we shifted our focus from the conventional marketing or finance-based focus to a materials resource based focus. In no way does it mean that we are to ignore these business functions. While our focus continues to be on these and other functions, we are looking at the possibilities or opportunities that can arise if we focus on the materials resources. In fact, this focus will help ease the marketing operations.

The focus on the materials resource, besides other benefits, helps marketing the most. The entire MRD department is organized and set up to respond to each and every marketing requirement in terms of cost base for quotations, technical support for securing potential customer orders, improvements/modifications in present products, development of new products, working on cost reductions to make the product competitive in the market and, most important of all, to deliver all marketing orders on time.

The marketing department need not follow up with various functions in the organization to know the stages (such as delays or delivery dates) of their various orders as MRD will be one-point contact for all the marketing orders. As we will see, even the shipping and customer- related problems will be handled by MRD.

There is no need to stress that marketing is the feed point for any business organization. Marketing is expected to function like a river - always flowing forward. Sales orders must be always flowing into the organization to keep the unit alive and working. It's a very important activity. Therefore, the marketing department's efforts, energy, charisma, knowledge and intelligence must be used in market research, market surveys, gathering market intelligence, increasing market share and increasing profit margin.

It must keep an eye on the future in terms of changes in technology, customer requirements and perceptions, and competitor's moves, as well as political developments and economic forecasts. It must alert the organization in time to modify present products or develop new products to widen its market base as well as remain competitive in the market.

The MRD concept enables the marketing department to focus on the main 'organization-sustaining' role of marketing to ensure continuous orders and being alert to the present and future market conditions and developments. How MRD enables marketing, I will explain now.

We defined the marketing role as an intangible materials resource activity. Therefore, it need not get into the physical servicing of its customers by way of delivery of products and post-sales activities, services and issues. This activity will be carried out by sales department, which, as we classified earlier, is a tangible material resource activity and goes under MRD.

Sales, as a part of the MRD team, will look into the physical fulfillment of the customer orders brought in by marketing. As mentioned earlier, marketing will secure orders from their customers and pass them to the MRD head. The MRD head, along with his team of manufacturing, engineering, sales and logistics and cost accountants, reviews the customer order to make sure that the technical specifications, manufacturing capability and commercial terms mentioned in the order/contract are understood and agreeable. MRD then takes the next step to plan for materials and to schedule production.

Sales, as part of the MRD team, is fully involved in the process of reviewing, readying themselves for production of the customer order. Once produced and packed, sales takes over for delivery to customer. Sales ensure payment collection and resolving quality issues and are responsible for customer relationship management. We will see more of their function under the tangible group.

Thus, as mentioned earlier, marketing under the MRD concept need no more run after manufacturing and other departments for servicing its customers in terms of order scheduling, delivery, customer complaints, collection of payments receivable, or even customer relationship management to a large extent. All this will be managed by MRD through sales.

With the one-point contact through the MRD head, marketing can update itself on the status of all their customer orders and assist MRD staff in case of any customer-related issues that go beyond the control of MRD. Marketing must only stay in touch with their customers to maintain relationship to ensure future orders.

An obvious question that comes to mind is how marketing will handle product development and conception of new products.

This is a high level and important aspect that will also involve the CEO of the organization. Many times it will be the CEO who will come up with plans and ideas for development of the existing products or introduction of new products. This is one of the important responsibilities of the CEO as he or she has to ensure the organization's market competitiveness, growth and perpetuity.

Product improvement/development or development of new products comes under R&D, design and development and the engineering departments. These are functions that deal with materials. Hence they fall under MRD. The MRD head, along with his respective development engineer, marketing and CEO, form a part of the team that will look into such developmental aspects.

It is a great advantage to have the R&D team under MRD, as every aspect of product development is a team effort and the MRD has all the essential members such as manufacturing, engineering, materials, sales, quality control to enable coordination so the development is implemented quickly and practically. R&D continues to take the lead in its development activities as approved by the CEO. The MRD head supports all such activities by providing help and support required from materials, engineering and manufacturing for R&D to carry out their development activity. This support will speed up the evolution as well as enable R&D to develop a more practical product since all functions involved in the development process will make it easier for moving the product into mass production once the process is complete.

In many cases, we find the development team, such as R&D, working in isolation and all the allied functions such as manufacturing, engineering or materials facing practical problems in terms of materials, specifications, or processes when the new development goes in for mass production.

MRD will enable a successful product development as they will 'begin with the end in mind', one of Stephen R. Covey's seven habits from the book, Seven Habits of Highly Effective People.

As mentioned above, MRD will free our marketing professionals from routine activities of customer order fulfillment, follow up, and other related activities and help them to focus on their core activity of marketing i.e. acquiring customer orders for the organization. As I mentioned earlier, with this, the power of focus starts working for the marketing department. Once they are free from routine activities of following up for order execution and attending to customer calls for delivery and complaints, marketing focuses on their prime responsibility of securing orders for the organization. They are bound to get more orders and the organization is bound to grow. That's the power of focus!

FINANCE:

While explaining the MRD concept, you will recollect that we had illustrated a hypothetical case in which finance was one of the partners of the IMRC, the Intangible Material Resource Corporation. Hypothesis apart, finance truly plays the role of an investor in an organization on behalf of the owner or owners of the enterprise. This is because it arranges all the required funds for the business from the banks, the owners, or the stakeholders and expects return on investment by way of profits.

Finance keeps track of all income and expenses of the organization through its Profit & Loss accounting and computes various financial ratios which enable the finance head, CEO and the owners of the organization to check the financial health of the organization on a regular basis.

They highlight the deviations in the annual budget on a monthly basis which helps the CEO to implement timely corrective actions and by highlighting cash receivables, finance follows up with marketing for cash receivables from the debtors of the organization to maintain the organization's liquidity. Finance also monitors all the assets of the organization and records its value in the balance sheet. It also tracks the rate of return on various investments the organization makes in the course of business.

The finance department's responsibility and importance is much greater than may be evident in the few points mentioned above. I have stated these points to show the basic functions of finance in relation to an organization's day to day functioning and help us understand how MRD can help finance in these aspects.

Firstly, as mentioned earlier, there is a need to have an accountant in the MRD department. This is because an accountant working on the shop floor with the engineers and various departments such as materials and sales can understand cost and works accounting much better and will have practical first hand information to relate to the cost aspect of what is happening in the plant. It is essential because MRD is responsible for the four aspects of the cost of a product and that is: material cost, process cost, labor cost and overhead costs. The accountant will help the MRD head to compute accurate costing and thereby inform marketing and CEO of the right cost to enable them to price the product accurately for their customers.

The accountant will also help MRD to track the ROI of all investments being made so that they can continuously work on ensuring the ROI as targeted or budgeted. This will also enable accurate tracking of the maintenance cost, production down-time cost and wastage of materials and utilities. In other words, we are trying to have an expert from finance to track accurately all related costs that will reflect correctly in the Profit & Loss account which is helpful for finance as well as MRD.

Besides the cost accountant, the next important way that MRD can aid finance is by having an accountant who will account for all the incoming materials as well as all outgoing products to the customer. The Invoices of the suppliers will be approved by this accountant in MRD based on the receiving system and procedures of the organization and approve all payments to the vendors based on documented receipts. The final payment will be issued by finance.

By handling the accounting of incoming materials, the MRD accountant will be able to closely interact with purchasing, incoming logistics and customs and ports clearing agent to compute the correct landed costs of input materials so essential for the final pricing of the product.

For all dispatches made by sales to the customers, the invoices to the customers will be raised by the accountant in MRD. Sales will follow up for all payments from the customers.

MRD will be responsible for all the assets of the organization, which we have already defined as the material resources of the organization and will be responsible for its upkeep and maintenance.

Therefore, as MRD freed marketing from routine activities of following up with various departments to fulfill their customer orders, MRD also frees finance from having to account for all the receipts and dispatches, cost accounting, following up for cash receivables, and keeping track of all the assets of the organization.

However, finance must coordinate closely with the accountants in MRD to ensure that all finance accounting principles, systems and procedures are adhered to. Finance must conduct half yearly financial audits on MRD with regard to purchasing, sales and all other accounting aspects that MRD carries out related to material resources.

Finance must also appoint an external independent agency to carry out technical audits to ensure that MRD is operating the technical aspects of the MRD function in line with accepted and expected engineering norms.

Thus, with the financial and technical audits, we ensure that MRD functions technically and commercially as per expectations and is doing justice to the major role it plays in the organization.

This means that the transactional nature of material accounting becomes the responsibility of MRD and finance needs to ensure availability of funds for supplier payment and to receive credits from customers. As mentioned earlier, MRD will have an accounting expert we shall call a materials accountant for these transactions who will be well versed with the practical aspects of procurement and sales transactions. This accountant will also do costing work related to landed cost of materials purchased and sold as well as process costs.

When materials transaction accounting is removed from the finance department, major accounting work will be freed from finance. The finance officer can then fully focus on financial acumen and routine activities such as financial statements, other investments, audits, finance-related legal aspects, etc.

HUMAN RESOURCE DEPARTMENT (HRD):

By its similarity, MRD sounds like some relative of HRD!

HRD has come a long way since the days it evolved onto the management scene and changed the function of what was then called the personnel department. The personnel department had a limited role and it had one wing called the time office. This office maintained the log book of all the employees reporting time and attendance to enable finance to provide monthly salaries to the employees.

The evolvement of HRD changed this limited role and now, besides recruitment and salaries, their primary responsibilities are the development of human resource abilities/capabilities, and improving the work environment, culture, and human relationships.

There are three major resources in an organization. They are human, finance and, of course, the materials resource. There is one more resource within the human resource heading and that is the intellectual resource. All organizations survive, grow and prosper based on the intellectual resource. This is a very important aspect that distinguishes one organization from the other within the same industry and makes it more competitive than the others. MRD recognizes this very vital resource for its success.

The intellectual resource can be further differentiated into technical and managerial. Technical refers to the knowledge and skill of any employee--be it an engineer, salesman, accountant or a buyer- -to perform any job. Managerial aptitude refers to the ability of any employee who, besides possessing technical intellect, can rise up to supervise and manage functions and other employees and also lead individual or multiple functions or even lead an organization in the future.

Basically, you will find three types of employees: high-, average-, and low-performing employees. The high performing employees take initiative and often do more than what is assigned to them. The average ensure that they do their allotted work in a timely and correct manner and the low perform at a level lower than expected in terms of speed and accuracy. In addition, we will also have under-performing employees, too.

The adequate presence or deficiency of these two intellectual resources i.e. technical and managerial resources in an organization, reflect the efficiency or deficiency level of the human resource. It is for the organization to decide at what level the technical or managerial intellect should break even. If the ratio falls below a particular level, the performance of the organization starts declining, other things being equal.

In case an organization is in a seller's market, average-performing marketing personnel will be enough to ensure continuity of orders. However, if the organization is in a buyer's market, then it is only the high-performing marketing personnel who can get orders for the organization and ensure its survival.

It is the standards of the organization that determine this composition of the intellectual level of an organization. The required composition will vary from organization to organization and they must have their own method to calculate this level. Again which jobs require what level of intellectual capability has to be decided by the organization. This identification helps HRD to arrange necessary training for various types of employees as required to maintain a high level of intellectual activity.

Once identified, the entire responsibility of the human resource department is to keep increasing the ratio of the Efficient (E) as compared to the Deficient (D) intellectual resource of employees at the highest level possible.

E > D is a healthy situation for any organization to perform well. The higher the ratio of E to D, the better the organization can be expected to perform from a job performance point of view. Training must be identified for the employees who are lackadaisical intellectually to raise the expected level, the failing of which will make them a liability for the organization.

A situation where E = D means HRD must arrange training to increase the level and make E > D. It may also need high caliber new recruitments to raise the standards and retrenchments of underperforming employees.

If an organization reflects E < D, and they do nothing in response to this, it may lead to the organization's failure. This is because, even if the organization is able to maintain and survive the present market competition and condition, as competition increases and market conditions change, the competitors will increase their own ratio of E to D. Then owing to its inability to intellectually respond to the challenges, this organization will fail. This is very critical for marketing, design and engineering and manufacturing.

On the other hand, even if the ratio of E > D does not guarantee an organization's success, it can still fail if the CEO or a group of individuals, like the top management executives, do not perform.

At the top management level, besides the intellectual levels of technical and managerial knowledge, the most important quality of all is leadership intellect. One of the qualities of leadership is to respond firmly in the event of a crisis, to face the challenge and find and implement solutions to rectify the situation. The other important quality of a leader is to foresee such problems or challenges.

Many organizational heads and executives fail on this count, which leads to the downfall of the organization. Their technical, managerial and leadership intellect does not match the requirements to meet the challenge or crisis. Their personal E is greater than D but when the challenges come their E > D did not matter as they were found deficient regarding leadership qualities. They did not 'sharpen their saw' to remain in business as one of the seven Habits requires us to do in Stephen Covey's book on Seven Habits of Highly Effective People.

HRD must ensure continuous practical training to the employees to brush up their knowledge in their respective fields. Attendance at seminars and such can update them with current practices in the industry and business world.

HRD's main role is to provide MRD with qualified human resources for the nature of jobs required by MRD. Under the MRD concept,

HRD will support MRD through their core functions of recruitment, retention, retrenchment, training and promotions as recommended by MRD, Marketing and Finance. All HRD policies, legal and industrial dispute matters, attendance and salaries will be the responsibility of HRD. Company legal matters and administration matters such as attendance, salaries, and housekeeping is under HRD.

For HRD, MRD becomes their internal customer and they have a great responsibility toward ensuring the successful performance of MRD.

'THE UNLEARNING CURVE'

We are all aware of the 'Learning Curve' which means that as we repeatedly do a job in the right way, we gain more proficiency in the same, based on which we increase our productivity. This is what helps CEOs and organizations to succeed. The CEOs take a particular objective for the organization and work toward it with their personal, technical, and managerial skills. This success quotient is translated downward in the organization. As long as the CEO's actions and the employees' actions are in the right direction, with other aspects such as business environment being equal, the organization continues to improve its proficiency in its business functions as a result of the learning curve.

When the CEO, a key function manager, or employees (it may be an operator of a key process, too) changes function or leaves the organization, it alters the way an efficient process or function was being carried out. This then starts the 'unlearning process' till such time as the new person can get back to the level of the earlier proficiency. For an unknown period the proficiency level attained is lost.

This is where succession plans or the 'bench strength' place a crucial role for all levels in an organization. Again, as mentioned in the case of the intellectual levels, the organization has to work out its own plan. High turnover of employees, managers and frequent changes at the top management keeps an organization in the 'unlearning curve' phase. E > D helps to maintain the learning curve. HRD has an important role to play in this respect.

HRD AND ENVIRONMENT:

In terms of MRD, HRD has a very major role to play in terms of materials resource conservation and environmental protection. It should ask for a percentage of the organization's profit to be provided for this cause. HRD must then take the initiative to align with social groups such as NGOs and other social service-minded organizations that work on natural resources conservation and environment protection projects to contribute to this noble cause.

MRD must help to contribute to such causes based on their own practical experience, successes and technical knowledge to contribute to the business fraternity in the form of social work to make the earth a better place to live. Just imagine, if all the HRD and MRD departments were to contribute to this social work of environmental protection, how quickly we could gain control of our polluting industries and businesses and start 'greening' again.

PENNY-WISE POUND-FOOLISH ATTITUDES MUST STOP:

HRD must take a very serious view regarding their organization's participation in sponsoring events that waste our natural resources in any form. Let me take the example of the annual Indian Premier League international cricket tournament which is played in India and now is in its fifth anniversary. This is a series of cricket matches that are played for almost a month during the evening under floodlights. Now just imagine the consumption of electric energy during this period; it might well run into the millions of watts. What is the necessity of playing a tournament in the evenings for over a month when this game can be played during the day? While you may have a few concluding games in the evenings, is it not a colossal waste of energy that takes place over a month? There are so many similar instances and examples of energy waste across the globe. Then why do we have 'earth day' and Save Energy slogans if we businesses waste energy? How can we then expect ordinary citizens to curb their use of electricity for normal day-to-day use. It is not 'walking the talk'. This is what I call the 'penny wise and pound foolish' attitude.

Even in organizations and corporations, senior management has a similar attitude. There will be a lot of control and curbing of low expense items such as, say, the use of office stationery to save costs to such a point in which sometimes employees are even constrained in their level of accomplishment. On the other hand, thousands of dollars and valuable time are spent on useless travels, seminars, meetings, consultants and dinners (where half the food is wasted and is not only a natural resource waste but also a crime if we consider the dire famine and neediness of some African and other underdeveloped countries today).

HRD, under the MRD concept, is expected to be an eye opener for the organization and direct its attention to also contribute to society. HRD must look into such aspects from a local and global point of view and make profit-making organizations contribute for global causes such as removing hunger and poverty and contributing toward the development of such needy nations.

It is gratifying to note that NGOs (Non-government organizations) across the globe are able to arrange funds in the millions and have devoted volunteers who work for such developments. Their contribution is much more significant than the governments which are stuck in bureaucratic mire and political wrangling. We, the business fraternity, can definitely contribute some funds and efforts for such noble causes.

Having seen the functions of the intangible group, we have to now look at the functions of the tangible materials resources group under the MRD concept. However, before that, we need to look at the person who will head the MRD function. The MRD head has the major responsibility to organize the MRD department and make the whole team play to meet the business goals of the organization. Therefore, we will now see this role in the next chapter.

CHAPTER 4

The MRD Head

BEFORE WE PROCEED to the functions of the tangible group under the MRD concept, which is the MRD department itself, it is necessary for us to understand the person who will lead the MRD department. What are the qualifications and qualities required to handle such a huge responsibility?

This will also help us to relate to the functions and responsibilities of the tangible group or the MRD department and the role of the MRD head as he takes charge of the department.

The MRD Head is a high profile job and assumes very high responsibility. Therefore, the MRD head's profile requires the person to possess a high level of technical, managerial and leadership qualities.

He is also the hero of the MRD concept as the implementation of this concept is in his and his department's hands. Therefore, it is important to elaborate his role, responsibility and characteristics to ensure success of this concept.

TECHNICAL AND MANAGEMENT QUALIFICATIONS:

The MRD Head is required to possess technical qualification in the field of business in which his organization is engaged. This is important because the MRD head is required to understand the complete technical functionality of the entire plant, its technology, product design, and manufacturing.

Thus, if we take the example of a firm that manufactures automobiles, then the MRD head, with a qualified automobile engineering qualification, will be able to understand the plant technology, automobile design, parts manufacture, and assembly line better.

Besides this, he should have years of practical experience in this field in various areas of the engineering aspect of the plant. This will enhance his understanding of the plant and equipment operations, product designing, maintenance and all types of materials required for the manufacture of various automobiles the firm produces.

The MRD Head has to lead and coordinate the functions of engineering, manufacturing, Sales and materials. He has to plan, direct, guide and make decisions on a day to day basis, short and long term to ensure the organizational goals and the MRD concept requirements are met. Hence, practical knowledge and good insight and foresight pertaining to the technical aspects are a must.

The MRD head is also required to have business management qualifications to understand all aspects of business. The MRD head not only handles the technical functions but also handles the commercial aspects of materials and sales. He should have good knowledge of finance in order to ensure that financial aspects related to the MRD department are carried out wisely. This includes issues of budgeting, profit and loss accounts, materials accounting, handling debtors and creditors, as well as other activities.

He also has administrative and managerial responsibilities in the MRD department. A practical knowledge for overseeing such commercial activities is again necessary to be able to direct these functions.

By the above, it appears that the MRD head should be a 'Know All' business management person. This is necessary because the MRD head's main responsibility is to put the MRD concept in place. As already seen, the responsibility of MRD is a very enormous one and is central to the performance of the business unit – profitably, at that. The person in charge must therefore be a person who has an understanding and practical knowledge of all the functions under the MRD department i.e. procurement, warehousing, inventory control, marketing and sales, manufacturing, operations, engineering (all aspects of engineering), finance, logistics and general management. Besides this, he must possess very good leadership qualities.

Therefore, this position is very unique. Now how does one find such a person in your organization, if available?

You will find that in your respective organizations, there will be one or two individuals at management/middle management levels who are qualified, knowledgeable –jack-of-all-trades type. They take initiative for assignments within and even out of their scope of responsibility, are problem-solvers, dependable, good coordinators, have good management skills, nurture good interpersonal relationships, and should have been working with the unit for quite some time. These are ideal candidates suited to be developed for this position.

As the concept is new, and the requirement so specific, we need to have a separate management course devised to develop MRD professionals who can head the MRD departments. The course will be required to cover MRD functions of various types of industries from a technical and business vantage point regarding engineering, operations, manufacturing, materials (procurement, warehousing, logistics), marketing, sales, finance. Leadership assets in psychology, philosophy and spirituality can also be vital.

While you may agree about having technical and management courses for the MRD head from a leadership perspective, I hope you will also agree with psychology and philosophy as part of the course. However, you may wonder what spirituality has to do with an engineering and management professional!

MRD HEAD LEADERSHIP QUALITIES:

Well, friends, spirituality is all about your spirit to live, be happy, make others happy, to enjoy, to create, to perform and help others perform, to trust and be trustworthy, be loyal, be cool, calm and composed, be a team player, be a leader who does justice to himself and others. And overall, it's nice if this individual has an appreciation for mother earth – our natural wealth and environment.

Now who says business management or technical professionals should not be made aware of or possess such beautiful attributes and qualities? Why should these qualities be alien to business professionals? All our problems of cheating, corruption and misappropriation in business will vanish if such qualities become a part of the business professional's culture. All this happens through a sense of 'spirituality' which helps us appreciate the value of human beings and Mother Nature and everything associated with it in business.

Let us understand that the owners, employers or the stakeholders of organizations trust professionals with their money for running a successful business. It is these entrepreneurs or stakeholders who give us our bread and butter. Therefore, for us, the business professionals, it becomes our paramount duty to fulfill that trust and faith with utmost sincerity and integrity.

We go asking for jobs and we solemnly pledge in our CVs to our prospective employers that 'I will discharge my duties to the best of my abilities.' But once we are in and get set in the organization, we tend to relax and take our positions for granted. We become critics and, when dissatisfied, do only the 'allotted job'—nothing more! We even spread our negative attitude to other employees.

My simple principle is that, if we are dissatisfied with our employers, we must try to improve the situation in whatever positive way possible by approaching the higher management in-charge. If everything is right with you, but the organization is a 'deaf' one, do not stay for a day more. You are worthy of better culture and organization with your leadership qualities.

But as long as you choose to stay, work every moment to give back to the employer what he is paying you for. Also ensure that you do all the activities that are required of you as a team member. Do not take a single dollar without performing your duties.

The cardinal principle of the MRD concept is that, we are all directly or indirectly concerned with material resources in an organization. Every act of ours either maintains the material resources or enhances the productivity of our material resources. A negative attitude and thoughtless work depletes the material resources in some way or the other every day and slowly leads the organization to fail. This we must never do.

Be it the intangible group or the tangible group, every employee that fails in this regard, from the CEO who misappropriates financial statements to the security guard who allows unauthorized material to be disseminated cause, not only small businesses, but also multinational and huge corporations to fail.

You will now appreciate my reasons for stressing not only the qualities of the brain and the intellect but also the qualities of the mind and heart that is our conscience.

You see, the MRD head will be entrusted with the entire materials resources of the organization. Added to that, MRD will give him human resources to utilize and convert the material resources into the end products of the organization. Those who utilize and convert resources are human beings first and employees second.

The leader must make the best use of his technical, management, philosophical and psychological knowledge to use the materials and human resources to the best of his ability. This means that, while he gets the optimum out of the material resources from an engineering and management angle, from a 'spiritual angle', through his integrity, he must ensure that he does not waste the natural resources from mother earth, directly or indirectly, nor does he pollute the beautiful environment of Mother Nature.

Secondly, the MRD head develops the MRD department into a place of performance and satisfaction that gives internal joy to every employee of the organization. This motivates them to return to work every day and stay with the organization till such time as retirement or such. These employees should never leave an organization because they do not enjoy the work, the supervision, or because the spirit, culture and the leadership within the organization has failed them.

THE MRD PROFESSIONALS:

Having explained about the role, qualifications and personal qualities of the MRD head, let me now explain to you the requirements of his team members in the MRD department.

Obviously, as you would imagine, based on the high profile requirement of the MRD head, you will expect the MRD team members also to be well versed in technical, management and leadership qualities!

If it was already so when you arrived, that would be great!

However, typically, if MRD is a new concept, it will require separate courses for developing professionals working in the MRD department, too.

The reason is that, the job in the MRD department requires the employees to work on multiple tasks and responsibilities and not be of a single track mind. Although specialists are a must, they should also be able to understand the functioning of the other departments. This is because we are now breaking the barrier of departments and therefore a procurement professional will be expected to work not only as a procurement specialist but also involve himself in the manufacturing, engineering, design, research and development, customer relationship management, accounting and other aspects within the MRD department role and responsibilities. An engineering professional must understand materials, manufacturing, sales function to be able to be part of the team and contribute. Similarly, other professionals in the MRD department are expected to function. Therefore, a course needs to be devised that trains every MRD professional on the essentials of 1) their role, 2) general ideas on certain industry processes that they wish to work in, 3) general technical and business management aspects that are common to all industries, 4) leadership qualities, all of which will help them carry out their responsibilities as effective team members.

The basic idea of MRD is to break the department barriers and have 'all rounder' professionals who can work in any area in the MRD department after being trained in this field and after a few years of experience. This will also result in developing leaders to head the MRD departments in the future.

You will now remember the 'all rounder' concept which I mentioned earlier, by example of the captain of a football team. The captain will be very happy if he gets players who can play in any position on the field. He can maneuver his players' positions anytime during play to enable him meet his plans and strategy on the field. Similarly, the MRD head will feel the flexibility with 'all round' capabilities of MRD professionals in his team.

'TECHCOMPHI' PROFESSIONALS:

Today, the trend with technical professionals is to obtain a business management degree. The management degree helps the technical individuals to have knowledge of the management and commercial aspects of all functions of the organization. Therefore, we have what we call the techno-commercial employees. This is a requirement today based on the commercial aspects that have pervaded the function of the engineer's job profile as they are required to work out project feasibility studies, ROI in case of purchase of new machinery and other finance- and commercial-related matters within their area of operations. Under MRD we are looking at this aspect as well as developing them to understand other business functions also.

In addition to the Techno-commercial requirements, of late, various philosophical aspects have now been brought into management. One example is Total Quality Management- [TQM] which stresses, for example, philosophical aspects such as 'Do it right the first time'.

Stephen Covey's book, The Seven Habits, was greatly acknowledged by the management world and professionals gained benefits from this book which reflected on their business practices in terms of their behavior and attitude. 'Begin with the end in mind' or 'Think win-win' are habits with great philosophical meaning and, when put into practice, offer great success in our business dealings.

Therefore, a time has now come for our techno-commercial professionals to also imbibe the philosophical aspects into their repertoire. This will make them highly successful. Hence, I call the new generation of business professionals 'TECHI-COM- PHI' i.e. technically, commercially and philosophically oriented.

It is this new generation of 'Techcomphi' professionals that are ideally suited for becoming MRD professionals as they will have the right criteria or the multifaceted requirements of the MRD professional. Other than this, the MRD professional will require training in industry- specific technical and management training to understand other business functions typical to the business organizations or industry for which they work.

MRD HEAD V/S the CEO:

Going by the qualifications required for a MRD Head, you may wonder whether we are asking for qualifications that are much more than the requirements of a CEO or are we actually making the CEO redundant!

The CEO is no doubt also a 'know – all' person heading the unit. He will have business and technical knowledge of his organization as well as the industry to which his organization belongs. However, his experience may or may not be practical, hands-on experience of the various business activities in the organization. He might be a specialist in one of the fields or possess a general knowledge of all the business functions based on years of experience in leading organizations.

The MRD function is different from that of the CEO in the sense that, with a fair knowledge of marketing, finance and HRD, the MRD man is expected to have technical qualifications and practical, hands-on experience of all the functions mentioned under MRD, manufacturing, and engineering the failing of which, he cannot do justice to the job.

The CEO's is a leadership job which involves setting goals for the organization, charting the way to meet these goals and coordinating the unit's activities toward this goal. His time is precious and therefore time and effort must be focused on business development, growth, profitability and organization's perpetuity.

The CEO's job is an upstream job which means he gets business into the organization and coordinates the top level activities of the organization without having to get into the day to day activities of ensuring the orders of the customers are delivered. While ensuring profit, the main responsibility of the CEO is to ensure the perpetuity of the organization through continued growth in the same area of business or new areas. As I see it, the CEO's goal should be to see what better organization he can hand over to his successor when he leaves. This will reflect his success during and after his tenure.

Under the MRD concept, the CEO's job is made easier to the extent that the CEO needs to coordinate with only the heads of marketing, finance, MRD and HRD to ensure that the organization's routine activities are going on as required. He can delve deeper into any business function if he sees signs that require his personal attention.

The MRD head's job is a transactional one and requires the person to get involved in the day-to-day activities of the entire MRD function. Therefore, practical knowledge of all these activities is a must.

Besides technical and commercial knowledge, as mentioned earlier, the MRD man has to be an excellent manager and a leader who has good knowledge of psychological and philosophical aspects of human nature. Besides this, there must be a spirit of love for Mother Nature and a dedication to avoid wastage of her natural resources and avoid polluting the beautiful environment. While this is true for the CEO also, the MRD person will be directly in charge of the human and material resources and 'working with his hands' he has more direct responsibility to make this happen.

MRD HEAD: GETTING STARTED

Let us now see how the MRD head takes charge of a unit under the MRD concept.

Having created the position of a MRD leader, his first responsibility is to own the entire materials resource under him. The function starts with the MRD head first organizing all the material-resource handling departments under its wings. They are procurement, warehousing, manufacturing/operations, engineering, sales, logistics and allied materials control activities such as quality control, safety and environmental. Heads of these respective functions, along with their respective team members, now administratively and functionally report to the MRD head.

His prime responsibility will be to deploy all the material resources at his disposal to produce products at a profit in view of the sales price of the product, optimum use of the material resources, material waste avoidance (for they are scarce and continuously depleting) and avoidance of polluting the environment in any form.

Besides the departments of each function now under MRD, it also collectively becomes responsible for all raw materials, WIP, finished stocks, pending purchase orders and sales orders, all in-bound and out-bound materials and products in transit, all machinery and equipment, the plant building, facilities, furniture and vehicles along with the respective human resources. It is now in a position to take over its main job of servicing marketing's requirements and ensuring ROI to finance.

In the following chapter, we will look at the functions of the tangible resource group comprised of manufacturing, engineering, sales and materials.

CHAPTER 5

MRD In Action - The Tangible Group

In the last chapter we saw the roles and responsibilities of the man responsible to handle the MRD department.

Now, we will see how the Tangible group, the MRD department, will work under the MRD concept.

Before we look at the functions of the MRD department, let us just review the four major paradigm shifts we have seen in the last chapter that are essential to the MRD concept.

1) We reorganized the organization from a conventional organizational set up to a material resource focused organizational structure.

The organizational structure is now based on the MRD concept of tangible and intangible material resource activities. The organization has now four major functions reporting to the CEO. They are marketing, finance, HRD (the intangible group) and MRD (the tangible group).

One advantage we saw in this structure is that the MRD becomes the CEO's one-point contact for all the organization's material resource related activities. This helps the CEO to be free from having to coordinate, review and direct so many other functions and resolve so many daily issues between departments and managers. This frees the CEO to focus on his major responsibilities toward the organization's overall performance, growth and profitability.

2) From marketing, we delineated sales and logistics activities to be placed under MRD function, as it is a tangible material resource activity. This makes MRD directly responsible to service the orders received from the customers. With this, MRD frees time for marketing from having to follow up with all

concerned departments in the organization for input to prepare quotations as well as service the customer's orders.

For marketing, too, MRD becomes the one-point contact for getting total materials and manufacturing cost of their product to quote to the customer's enquiries as well as delivery of their orders and after-sales services.

3) In case of finance, the materials accounting in terms of purchases and sales, which is typically a finance function, is shifted to MRD with a separate accountant under MRD. This is done as material accounting is an allied function of materials ordered and received and materials converted into finished product and dispatched to the customers. MRD will also advise finance on payments to suppliers based on approved material, received documents, as well as follow up with customers for payments. This frees finance from a major portion of their routine activity of supplier and customer receipts and sales accounting.

Similarly, cost is also under MRD because the person involved in costing must be on the shop floor to understand the exact physical and transactional nature of the cost aspects he is trying to work out.

This helps the MRD head to keep close track of the input costs in terms of materials and process as well as any financial aspects such as ROI on investments, etc.

Therefore, as in the case of CEO and Marketing, MRD frees finance from the day-to-day routine activities of material-related accounting. They can focus on higher level of finance functions for the organization.

4) In case of HRD, MRD expects HRD to work with it closely to keep the ratios of $E > D$ (Efficient Intellect employees' v/s Deficient Intellect employees) with appropriate all round training i.e. technical as well as personal development, and recruiting and keeping back-up or bench strength of genuinely qualified and capable professionals.

Thereafter, MRD expects regular trainings to keep the employees updated on current business best practices, new technologies, business trends and situations, as required, to the appropriate category of employees to ensure an intellectually vibrant organization.

Now, let me dwell a little on the meaning and thrust behind the three letters and words of the MRD **concept - MATERIAL, RESOURCE AND DEPLOYMENT.**

Materials stands for items **needed to create something.**

In the case of business, they represent all the input materials in raw, semi or finished form and assets which are all in material form. Therefore, under the MRD concept, the buildings, plant and machinery fall under materials.

The reason is, as explained earlier, we wish to focus on the tangible aspects of business with a material base and focus on its management. They form the physical resources for doing or carrying out business. Materials incur cost while acquiring them, incur maintenance costs, and enable businesses directly or indirectly to form an asset for the organization. Hence, with proper utilization, maintenance and longevity they aid the organization in its business performance. If proper focus is given to the material resources in an organization, it is a goldmine which can save costs and improve profits. Hence, MRD focuses on all material resources in the organization.

Resources can be explained as that which is used **to fulfill an intended material use.**

In case of business, it is the materials in all forms that we mentioned above, which we use in our day-to-day business. Materials help us in our manufacturing activity, trading activity or even in carrying out our service-oriented business. In other words, all such materials help us in their intended use and therefore become our resources to help us carry out our respective business goals and objectives.

Now, let me explain '**Deployment**' which stands for **using something effectively.**

In case of our business, under the MRD concept, we look at how well you can deploy the 'material resources' to enable us to conserve materials as well as save on environmental pollution issues while extracting, transporting, converting, storing, delivering to customers and when use is completed, enabling them to dispose of the same. The focus on deployment has to be such that we are able to make the best use of all the limited material resources.

In other words, the approach and attitude is to plan out deployment of the limited material resource in hand to the best of our business management ability while carrying out our business activities. When done properly, it will save costs arising out of wastage in any form, enhance productivity of all materials, schedule maintenance, avoid break down costs; and this will result in increasing the competitiveness of the organization, leading to more business and resulting in more profits. Simple, right?

THE ARMY AND MRD!

Although it may sound odd, we can draw some parallels between the MRD concept and the armed forces to enable me explain how important it is to look at the materials resource usage from an army's angle. There they have limited resources which demand excellent planning, coordination, and deployment to ensure victory.

The armed force typically consists of the Army, the Air Force and the Navy. They have limited manpower, the trained soldiers, deployed for all war-related activities. Besides this, they have limited ammunition and equipment such as military tanks, fighter aircraft, ships, submarines, etc. The chief of the armed forces is expected to maintain his forces and equipment and be prepared for war at anytime. He should know his enemies, potential enemies, and keep track of all neighboring and global developments that might lead to a war.

This is similar to our business scenario wherein we have limited resources within our organization and we are expected to be aware of our market, trends, and competitors and the organization must be ready to meet any changes required to beat competition and capture the market.

In the case of a war, the chief of the armed forces must be alert at all times, plan out his strategy to combat the enemy and decide the use or deployment of his forces and equipment in the best possible action to ensure victory with the least loss of forces and equipment. Both forces and equipment should last the duration of the combat.

During the war, he must strategize in the movement of his forces; and he must give them required materials, equipment and food. Besides this, he must ensure that communication of the plan and strategy goes down to every battalion in combat so that all of them fight in a coordinated effort.

This reflects our business scenario wherein the organization has to work on a daily basis, like the war, working to a strategy and plan, ensuring that every process (every move in case of the army) is right and we deliver the right product to the customers to meet their satisfaction (like the actions that bring victory for the army).

The function of the MRD head, under the MRD concept, can be compared to the chief of the armed forces in terms of optimum utilization of the limited material resources at his disposal to meet his goals.

The MRD head is in charge of limited resources for the manufacturing activity i.e. trained manpower- the employees, like the trained army. The input materials to convert into a product can be compared to the limited ammunitions which an army must use effectively to achieve the desired result –victory. For a manufacturing unit, of course, it means their output in sold product!

The plant, building, and equipment that help make the products are like the tanks, fighter aircraft, ships, submarines, control towers and bunkers that help soldiers fight war and achieve victory. Just as the army general strategizes and uses the Army, Air Force, and Navy effectively, so, too, the MRD head has to effectively deploy the engineering, manufacturing, sales and materials activities with related equipment and the manpower to meet the desired business goals.

The essence of what I am trying to convey is that, as in the case of war, victory has to be achieved with the limited resources in hand. Not a single bit of manpower, ammunition or equipment can be wasted; it demands the most sensible, logical and effective strategy for deployment of the resources in hand to ensure victory. In business, too, we should have the same attitude in regard to our limited material resources.

Just like the army general keeps himself and his army alert, prepared, and ready for a war anytime, the MRD head must maintain and keep his manpower and material resources ready to meet market demand, the latest technology and beat competition. Our organizations must have this attitude toward our material resources.

This approach will ensure a wise and prudent use of our natural material resources while manufacturing products, thereby conserving our resources and making, using and disposing of them in a manner not affecting nature negatively. This will also be a victory for our business fraternity. In the present situation of dwindling material resources and increasing environmental degradation by the business community, the MRD approach will help us focus and control these two burning global issues.

MRD DEPARTMENT:

Let us now focus on the four main tangible functions of the MRD department – manufacturing, engineering, materials and sales. All other tangible business functions will fall under one of these main functions.

Hitherto, these four functions were working as independent departments and were coordinated to the extent required. Each of them worked like the 'relay race,' doing their part and handing over to the next user what was required of them.

Thus, for example, if quality control checked the final products and gives a report of acceptance or rejection to manufacturing, it was then left to manufacturing to figure out what went wrong with the products that were rejected and take corrective action.

In case the rejection related to engineering or material problems, the same was notified to engineering by quality control and manufacturing and awaited corrective actions by the concerned party.

In daily routine activities, some problems are attended to or resolved immediately. The ones that require time, effort or decisions do not get resolved immediately. This is so because the concerned are busy with something more important in their respective department or they simply do not understand the importance of resolving the problem that awaits corrective action. Then there is the usual 'Come through my boss' or 'Let my boss instruct me'. When the problem is pushed up toward the higher management levels, it finally gets resolved. Many times the issue goes to the top management, like the CEO's level, after which a solution is found! In some cases one manager drags another to the CEO for a gala fight to decide whose job it is to solve the problem!

Such issues are a routine affair in our day-to-day work. This is because, as I mentioned earlier, when the 20 to 30% overlap activity, problem solution or decision comes across a desk, it becomes the case of the 'who will bell the cat'?

What happens in our current set up is that the CEO is the boss of all the various business functions in the organization. The managers of the respective functions report to the CEO. Now the CEO is not expected to look into the details of the day-to-day activities of the manufacturing and allied processes. He has other important areas related to the organization business performance and growth to focus on. He reviews the overall activities based on reports and meetings with the concerned heads of the various functions. However, all problems do not surface at the CEO's level. All problems that the heads of the various functions cannot find solutions for between themselves remain problems until resolved by the CEO. This affects the organizational performance. And by the time the problem is brought to the CEO's notice, the damage has usually been done.

We cannot blame the various function heads either. The department heads of these functions have their own goals, targets and objectives to achieve. On top of this, there are the other day-to-day 'urgent requirements' of the CEO. The focuses of these heads therefore become highly individualistic in nature out of no choice of their own, simply to ensure that they fulfill their role.

What is required is a holistic approach and a combined focus to meet the organization's objectives, budgets and goals through the optimum use of the material resources. This can be achieved once all these functions come together and work for a common goal with shared and common responsibilities under one head. A common head will be able to coordinate these four main activities between themselves, set the right priorities and work from an organized, centralized hub.

Therefore, the first goal of the MRD head is to identify such individualistic as well as common goals for the manufacturing, engineering, materials and sales function under the materials resource department.

In a general way, we can summarize the individual and common responsibilities of the four departments under MRD as follows:

MANUFACTURING:

Responsible for manufacturing the required products at optimum productivity levels, maintaining plant and machinery, optimum use of materials, energy conservation and meeting environmental protection requirements in process and wastage disposal.

Also responsible to work with materials for input material requirements, quality and supplier relationship with engineering for all technological support and with sales for customer delivery, quality and customer relationship.

ENGINEERING:

Responsible for maintaining complete plant and machinery, all engineering support to manufacturing, technical specifications of materials, equipment, machinery and plant and building requirements to materials and R&D, technological upgrades to meet energy conservation and environment protection needs, technical advice and support to materials, marketing, sales, suppliers and customers.

MATERIALS:

Responsible for providing materials and services to manufacturing and engineering by providing materials, machinery, equipment, plant and building requirements as specified. To ensure material, energy conservation and environment protection requirements of all procured goods and services. Responsible for working toward a high level of supplier relationship and with sales for high level customer relationship.

SALES:

Responsible for working closely with materials, manufacturing and engineering for the marketing orders delivery. Arrange packaging, transporting, in transit warehousing, handling and timely delivery of goods to customers through fuel/energy efficient and pollution conscious shipping agents. Ensuring high level customer relationship through timely delivery, Customer feedback to engineering, manufacturing and materials and providing solutions for the customer.

The above responsibilities, while indicating the primary responsibility of the concerned department, involves them and holds them responsible for meeting the functions of the other department.

Therefore, we have now corrected the individualistic approach of the departments by including in their responsibilities the expectations of the other departments. This means they are now responsible to work together to achieve a common goal functionally and administratively as they are now under one head, the MRD head. All professionals in the MRD department will have their job responsibilities on the above lines which would mean that they will have 60% responsibility toward their own function and 40% toward other's functions. This will complement a level of teamwork such that there will be individual performance as well as combined working to achieve a common goal of making oneself and others successful.

In keeping with our main aim of MRD, besides considering the most essential responsibilities here in case of manufacturing, engineering, materials and sales, we have laid stress on material and energy conservation, environmental protection and supplier and customer relationships which are the essence of the MRD concept. If these functions don't bring success, no one department can do it. And it can happen only under this coordinated set-up of the MRD organizational chart. What we often find are halfway attempts and the usual story of the 'coal calling the kettle black': manufacturing blaming engineering,

engineering blaming materials, and the round robin goes on... We must sincerely wish to drastically improve the business process, look at making more profits, and have serious concern for the material resources and the environment.

Let us now elaborate regarding the function of the MRD group based on these four major functions.

The MRD Head takes over charge of the MRD department. He becomes the "owner" of all the tangible material resources of the organization. As we defined earlier this includes the plant and building, machinery and equipment, materials and finished products. He leads the employees under the MRD department which includes the employees from the functions of manufacturing, engineering, materials, and sales.

The MRD head's main responsibilities are:

1) Taking ownership and responsibility of the complete material resources of the organization, its use and accountability.

2) Ensuring optimum use of the 'material resources' through effective deployment, working on continuous cost reduction, technological innovation in product development and manufacturing process that meets material, energy conservation and environmental protection standards and gives finance a good ROI.

3) Planning effective deployment and use of the material resources to enable and offer competitive costs to marketing related to materials, engineering, manufacturing and logistics of various products manufactured by MRD to enable marketing to decide on pricing of the products to their customers.

4) Manufacturing products at or below the quoted costs for marketing, meeting customer delivery time, delivering safely to customer site, meeting stated quality and intended use with installation and commissioning wherever required and ensuring after-sales services.

5) Developing and maintaining good supplier and customer relationship by working with them closely as extended arms of the MRD department and organization.

ROLE OF THE MRD DEPARTMENT:

The MRD Head will coordinate the responsibilities and activities of all the four departments. Here, the best advantage is that we now have all the so called 'warring functions' under one head. By warring what I mean is that the functions of engineering, materials, manufacturing and sales, being distinct, will never by themselves coordinate or cooperate with each other. The thinking is that 'I Know my job; you do your job', 'if you provide this… I will get that done…' 'They do not understand our problems…' etc…. These badly require a coordinator to get things done.

Now the MRD head looks at the four functions in unison and therefore becomes 'An Enabler' and will be able to plan, strategize and coordinate all functions to meet the desired goals. He can direct each function and make decisions on the spot. There is no need to wait for the CEO approvals and showdowns. In one meeting with the CEO, the MRD apprises him of the status, giving approval and making decisions wherever and whenever required.

To meet the above, some basic activities of the manufacturing, engineering, materials and sales functions can be mentioned as under:

MANUFACTURING:

This function has four major responsibilities:

1) To receive customer enquiries from marketing and quote for the same.
2) To receive from marketing customer orders and prepare the sales plan in coordination with materials, sales and engineering.
3) Help procurement in planning the material and coordinate with the vendors along with materials for any deviation in plan, schedule and improvement in vendor performance.
4) Manufacture to the customer needs considering the best use of the manufacturing facility.
5) Work closely with sales to ensure timely delivery to the customers.

Let us elaborate on the above:

Manufacturing, so to speak, is left to right or right to left function i.e. it receives the marketing orders and the input materials and service from one side, converts and delivers it to the other side, which constitutes the finished product. We can show the same diagrammatically as follows:

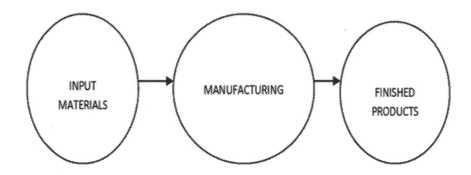

This explains that it is central to the function of the material conversion to finished product. It is dependent on supply management prior to conversion and responsible to sales management after conversion. Engineering helps by providing the right technology, well maintained machinery and equipment.

Under MRD, the MRD director receives the marketing orders. The orders are reviewed with the MRD team consisting of manufacturing, materials, engineering and sales. The best advantage in this system is that the orders get reviewed at one time with all the concerned functions and any clarifications can be sought for at this time.

In our present set-up the orders get reviewed individually by one function and many times the inconsistencies in the order come to light at the time of manufacturing. If they do not get highlighted, a wrong product gets manufactured leading to rejections by the customer.

The target here is to take into manufacturing all orders that are clear from this team point of view to ensure unhampered production. One of the first goals of manufacturing is to ensure the highest level of productivity and it is now possible, under MRD, for achieving the same, as all the concerned functions are now part of one team. This will streamline the timely flow of product to meet delivery commitments to the customer.

Manufacturing along with engineering must ensure that the plant, machinery and equipment are well maintained at all times to avoid any down time of production or loss of assets owing to deterioration. This aspect covers the main responsibility of the MRD head besides taking care that all material resources in any form in process avoids waste and ensures environmental care.

Quality control:

Quality control or quality assurance – the more proactive term includes:

1) responsibility to support procurement and suppliers in ensuring the right quality of in-put materials,
2) supporting manufacturing in producing products of the right specifications and
3) working with sales management to resolve customer complaints about quality and taking necessary corrective actions.

It works closely with engineering, manufacturing, sales, materials, suppliers and customers. The QC function is a virtual end to end function because QC has to assure quality from a supplier's supplier right up to customer's customer end. Being under one head, the MRD, quality assurance becomes a part of the materials and sales team and carrying out this responsibility becomes much easier. They play the most important role of training the suppliers for quality improvement and take all necessary actions on customer complaints.

Engineering:

Under MRD, engineering plays the central role in fulfilling the goals of the MRD concept. It is responsible for the right specification of input materials that will specify, as far as possible, environmentally friendly and biodegradable materials, work out specifications and usage that will minimize waste in terms of consumption, as well as identify production process wastages and protect the environment.

Similarly, engineering is expected to maintain the entire manufacturing facility including plant, building, machinery and equipment at an optimum usage condition. An engineering department's ability, capability and performance is reflected in the status of the technology in vogue in the manufacturing plant and the product produced. From MRD's main objective point of view, the engineering function is expected to reduce/re-use waste, and employ optimum utilization of the material resources –(plant, materials, machinery and equipment and process technology) to reduce or nullify environment pollution.

The R&D under engineering works for using green products and producing green products. Under MRD, it has direct responsibility as well as now being a part of manufacturing and procurement, and will be able to coordinate with these important functions to meet its objectives.

This function plays a technical support role to the entire MRD function. It is the center for technology and is expected to keep the organization informed regarding the latest in technology for manufacturing, material engineering and product development to enable the organization to maintain its market leadership.

Research & Development – R&D

Market research will warrant development of new products or development of existing products. This activity is carried out by the R&D department. R&D is a tangible materials resource activity and therefore will fall under MRD. There is a great advantage in having R&D under MRD.

Generally, in many organizations R&D is a separate department that works independently and is continuously engaged in product development activity. They do their own material purchase and have their own production facility. Once they develop a product, they hand it over to manufacturing for regular production.

One of the greatest drawbacks to such an R&D set-up is that they work on their own and make their own prototypes, and material procurement, and pricing of the product. When the developed product comes to online manufacturing, all types of problems surface regarding mass production and procurement of the new materials in terms of price, quantity, delivery time. These problems can offset all calculations made by the R&D team.

Under the MRD concept, R&D is given very high importance and will have direct access to materials market information and the manufacturing facility, as the MRD head will be directly coordinating the R&D efforts. In other words, all development will be an online development and therefore when the product is developed it has no gestation period for manufacturing. It can go on-stream straight away. So we not only have the 'early involvement of vendors' in the development activity but 'early involvement' of the entire MRD team, too.

Under MRD, it will get all the focus necessary (procurement/manufacturing and any other support services) to develop a product considering all three aspects: material specifications, prices and availability, manufacturing set-up and time factor for introducing the product into the market. (To some extent, even value engineering and value analysis can be carried out during the time of development itself).

Time factor is of great importance for a new or modified product to be introduced in the market. It can lose acceptability and lose over competition because of sluggishness, overshooting developmental costs and final product costs, leading to a failure in the launch of a new product.

Today, multinationals and large corporations also face the problems mentioned above, although they have a full fl edged R&D set-up. It is essential to have a developmental product integrated into the routine manufacturing system as early as possible to avoid an alien entering into the routine manufacturing set-up after its development has been implemented elsewhere. Moreover, the expertise of the routine manufacturing line personnel can help remove many production *teething problems* that usually become bottle necks later on.

Sales:

We have taken a revolutionary step to separate the sales activity from marketing. Marketing, as we considered under the MRD concept, is a high level function that plays the role of sustaining an organization as well as enabling its growth through continuous orders from the customers.

We therefore sum up that the main function of marketing as market research, market intelligence, market presence (market share, advertisements), sales orders, best pricing, and perpetuity (ensuring gradation of existing product as long as possible with timely replacement of new products for market). Marketing must focus on this activity.

We also found that, as it does not directly deal physically with the product it sells, it gets classified into intangible activity. The physical activity of delivering the finished goods we entrusted with sales. Therefore, as tangible activity it falls under MRD.

The role of sales management is, in a sense much larger than marketing in terms of their duty toward the customer. The onus of customer relationship management (CRM) falls under sales.

Sales play an important role during MRD's finalization of the manufacturing plan along with manufacturing, materials, and engineering. It's during this plan that the first step to customer satisfaction is taken care of in terms of timely delivery by appropriate scheduling. Sales follow up closely with manufacturing to take over the manufactured products for delivery to the customer. In case of any delay, sales is aware of the problems instantaneously and is therefore able to communicate to the customer of the delay and revised delivery schedule instead of keeping the customer in the dark and upsetting the customer. Sales can work on plans to change the mode of transport, to speed up the delivery or shorten the delay, if required.

The out-going logistics under sales has the responsibility of planning delivery right from the time the customer orders are received by MRD. This will help them work out the best prices for transport and save further on the quoted freight charges to the customer. It can work out inventory levels if it has transit warehouses or finished goods warehouses or distribution points within the state, country or in other countries. It can plan deliveries accordingly.

Sales will handle the debtors. For this reason sales will have an accountant in MRD who will prepare sales invoices and record all sales transactions as required under financial accounting. This will take the burden off finance to do accounting matters of sales. The sales department will follow-up for payments from the customers before or after delivery as agreed to with the customer by marketing.

Sales will also handle customer complaints in terms of product performance. The greatest advantage is that, as sales is a part of manufacturing, engineering, materials, R&D and quality assurance, the customer complaints get direct attention from these departments as needed.

The MRD head will review such problems with the team instantaneously and not only take corrective action for the customer but also immediately rectify the same within the organization for whatever cause, be it process, an engineering problem or a materials/ supplier problem. This is one of the greatest advantages of the MRD because the customer complaints do not just get piecemeal attention and remedy but all concerned personnel look at the customer complaint as a whole. In fact MRD takes the ownership of customer satisfaction. This is why we said earlier that the supplier and the customers become extended arms of the MRD.

We will look at this most important aspect of the entire MRD activity and that is – customer satisfaction and relationship in the next chapter. Another important aspect of the separation of sales from marketing is that sales will focus on the execution of the order in all respects including installation, erection and commissioning and after-sales service. All these aspects get reflected right at the time when the MRD supervisor reviews the order for execution. Therefore, all such activities get built into the system well in advance and therefore are executed in a timely and systematic manner.

Sales handles out-going transportation or outbound logistics A point that needs to be stated is that, under MRD, the ability, responsibility and performance of the MRD personnel will vary from the standard ones in order to meet the function and responsibility under MRD. Therefore, HRD must provide training as required to develop any new capability required. By handling transportation, sales need not depend on other departments in the organization for their delivery performance. Second, they can have direct control over the transportation cost, helping MRD to get the best rates, save costs, and show profits.

The concept of one logistics or transportation department has not been considered to enable the direct concerned users of transportation services to get their best rates. Therefore, the in-coming logistics will be handled by members of the procurement department themselves to enable them to have contact with their vendors or arrange transportation with any logistics service provider.

The MRD head, being the finalization authority, will always be able to decide on such areas where transportation interest can be combined for procurement and sales to set up joint transportation contracts wherever necessary. The proverbial saying goes that the left hand does not know what the right hand is doing. Under MRD, in this case, the right hand knows what the left hand is doing and they are literally under the control of one brain!

IT DEPARTMENT:

Information technology was a very specialized field in the 80s when it broke onto the business scene on a large scale. At first, computers were provided to a privileged few, were used in only air conditioned rooms and the operating system seemed too complicated for many to learn. All that was changed by Microsoft and today, more than twenty years later, computers are a part of not only our business but also our personal lives.

One of the fastest growing industries as well as educational fields, we have millions of computer-literate professionals today, graduated into hardware and software systems in such a short time. Schools and colleges have made computer learning a part of their curriculum and businesses require computer literate employees.

While IT software development has an endless scope, in industries, once an ERP solution is implemented in an organization, it does not require a different IT department to look after the IT needs of the organization. It requires only software and hardware maintenance services. Moreover, with automated plants and machineries which are all computerized, the IT's presence will be required more on the shop floor than in the administration buildings. Therefore, we can consider IT as an engineering activity like mechanical engineering and place the same under the engineering function.

Competent IT professionals in the IT department can develop their own MRD ERP.

HEALTH, SAFETY & ENVIRONMENT:

We will now look at the processes. About each process we ask: Is it environmentally friendly? This is one of the major concerns under MRD. Besides, they handle all safety related firefighting equipment and personal protection equipment. This is thus considered a tangible activity and therefore environment and safety become a part of the MRD team.

Under MRD, HSE becomes a proactive function that works along with the functions of manufacturing, engineering, materials and sales to make the MRD concept successful by finding solutions to avoid any non-compliance of HSE requirements. It's now a joint effort, not just the responsibility of the HSE to take care of or enforce.

Hence, engineering will find solutions along with manufacturing, Materials are used to improve the process capability to avoid waste in liquid, solid, or emission of gases through modifications to existing equipment, newer methods, or state-of-the-art technology. It now becomes a team goal under MRD to tackle pollution and waste in any form from within the plant.

If all organizations big or small, trading or services (their set-up should have 'green' concept) work under the MRD concept, there will be a direct focus by the business world on avoiding environmental degradation. This will cause concerted efforts from all manufacturers in reducing CO_2 emissions, which is one of the main goals of MRD, as the manufacturing industry is the chief pollutant.

MRD IN TRADING ORGANIZATIONS:

In trading, an organization 1) brings in products, 2) stores them in their warehouses, if required, 3) repacks or assembles and then 4) distributes them to retail stores or direct customers. The main operations are limited to the repacking or assembly. Therefore, the sales price includes not only the transportation cost (incoming and outgoing), but storage and, if applicable, re-packing/assembly charges.

The MRD concept works along the lines of a manufacturing unit and can be separated into tangible and intangible resources. Therefore, marketing, finance and HRD form the intangible group and the materials team (procurement, in-coming logistics and warehousing), operations (planning and execution of deliveries to customers by packing, repacking or assembly) and sales (delivering the products to retail stores, dealers or direct customers). The MRD head will coordinate with marketing to receive the requirements from marketing of their resale products. This, the MRD head will coordinate with their design/ engineering team (depending upon the trading company whether it deals in engineering or non-engineering products) or the technical expert of the product and decide about ordering from standard trading partners/principals or from the market. Upon receiving, arrange inspection by quality control, arrange storage, and then deliver to the customers through sales.

The MRD's main responsibility will be the same as in the case of a manufacturing unit, that is, to ensure that material resources in the form of the products ordered are improving the MS ratio on a continuous basis, good supplier relationship, inventory control, proper storage and handling of all products, efficient repacking, assembly and loading for timely delivery to customers, customer relationship management and customer after sales services.

The greatest advantage of MRD concept for the trading business is that it will now have an ownership of all its material resources that is, trading products, warehouses, handling equipment and office buildings under one head. Marketing focuses on orders, as it will be free from deliveries, and finance focuses on their prime financial responsibilities other than the purchase and sales accounting.

MRD IN SERVICE ORGANIZATIONS:

The service based organizations are very similar to the trading organizations as they will have limited operations. Let's take the example of a hospital. The main material resources will be the medical equipment and surgical instruments, medical supplies, the hospital buildings and facilities such as operation theaters, the furniture and warehouse.

The MRD head ensures that all the material resources are purchased of the right quality and best price and ensures upkeep of all the material resources as well as keeping track of the ROI for all the medical equipment.

From an operations point of view, his deliverable is good service to the out-patients as well as the in-patients. The part of his team will be materials, bio-medical (the engineering experts), maintenance and housekeeping. The MRD ensures positive supplier relationship with all its suppliers of medical equipment and medical supplies and ensures the customer relationship through customer satisfaction starting when the patients are in the hospital for treatment through providing all the doctors, nurses and supporting staff all their material-based requirements. This also involves storing in correct correct facilities and maintaining the same.

The MRD head must work toward the use of bio-degradable products, proper disposal of all wastes without polluting the environment and other 'green' practices to make his hospital a 'green" hospital

MRD FOR PRACTICING PROFESSIONALS:

MRD is applicable to even a lawyer or chartered accountant who run their own practices. For such business people, they are themselves the 'MRD head'!

Besides maintaining their main material resources, their office and furniture, they must take care of all office related or practice related equipment such as Xerox machines, computers and all other office supplies and stationery and use bio-degradable products such as bio-degradable printing cartridges. In other words, they must look at 'greening' their office and work environment.

MRD – RESPONSIBILITIES:

We have now seen a very broad function of the Tangible and the Intangible departments under the MRD concept.

Let me now broadly classify the basic area upon which an MRD department should focus, which I feel, based on the type of industry, will become applicable.

The MRD department will have all the tangible activities as part of their team. The four main activities manufacturing, engineering, materials, sales and other tangible activities under these activities will be termed functions. This is because, under MRD, we aim to create a seamless business process within the organization of the tangible activities. Therefore, by breaking down the department status of these main facets, we will remove the compartmentalization of these functions. The department classification was fine when management was evolving and specialized activities were separated to enable them to perform on their own and contribute their best for the organization.

Today, with the advances we have made in the science of management, we are seeing the link and overlapping of these main functions which can bring the best out only if they are brought to work together. In fact, the main cause of material wastage and environmental problems can be attributed to this fact, as what one department did was considered to be expert and the other department had no say in such matters and had to live with what was thrust upon them.

So if engineering designed a product, then it was taken as final. Manufacturing, materials and others rallied around it to make the production happen and surmounted problems as it came by them. Only when they created real problems were the problems brought to the forefront and solutions found.

Again, if engineering selected a technology for manufacturing, manufacturing had no choice but to use and produce from the given technology to the best of its ability. Obviously, manufacturing will claim no ownership of the problems of the technology and will be all out to blame engineering for the problem, be it productivity, technical shortcomings, wastage, rejections or environmental problems.

Today, thanks to the wide network and reach of education, technical and management qualifications, technical and commercial professionals in the organization are generally much more educated, trained and experienced as compared to the earlier generations. Therefore, although they might be specialists in their own fields, they definitely understand the overall functioning of the organization. Be it technical or commercial matters, they can all contribute toward diverse functions other than their specialized field. We are therefore aiming at synergizing the total knowledge by working as a team and sharing common goals and objectives within the MRD department to enhance performance of the organization.

Under the MRD concept, we are looking at creating all-round professionals who can work in any function within the MRD department, giving choice to the MRD head to maneuver his team members to any function as the situation demands. Just like the captain of the football team who has a few players who can play well in any position, it enables the captain to move his players around as the situation of the game demands.

PRIORITY FOCUS FOR THE MRD DEPARTMENT:

The responsibility of the MRD head is to meet the marketing orders with profit margin as committed and return on investments to finance.

Besides this, it has to meet the fundamental requirements of:

1) Conservation of material resources
2) Reduce/ avoid impact on environment

The MRD concept is expected to deliver the above. A few points that need focus on the part of the MRD department toward the material resources of the organization are as follows:

1) Conservation of material resources:

One of major concerns today is the dwindling natural material resources. Having mindlessly strip-mined the natural resources, the only choice we have now is to prolong its availability. This can be done by consuming less of the scarce resources and second, by avoiding use of the scarce resources and attempting to draw from the more abundantly available natural resources. For example, wherever solar energy can be used, petroleum products can be avoided. This will save the consumption of crude oil and extend its time of availability.

We should not consider curbing even a small quantity of consumption as insignificant because, when calculated at a global level of consumption, such quantity can add up to a huge quantity. Therefore, if one small organization with an innovation manages to save 10 watts of power every month, that 10 watt power savings when calculated over 10,000 other units in the same industry can yield a saving of 100,000 watts per month and annually this will work out to 1.2 million watts! This is the essence of the MRD concept – materials resource saving.

We have to look at every aspect of material resource consumption by business minutely and scientifically in order to arrive at the right resource and optimum utilization. As seen in the example, there are thousands of items which, when evaluated, will result in material resources savings in various industries and lead to millions of tons of reduction of material resources. This requires cooperative awareness right from the CEO to the R&D or engineering designer to every individual in the business process line to think how we can use less and wastage can be avoided at every stage from extraction, packing, transportation, product design, conversion, usage, re-usage and disposal. We will see how this works under the MRD concept.

The elementary reasons for material wastage in an organization are:

1.1) Defect in Planning:

Wastage of material out of poor or wrong planning is a waste contributed by the management.

To begin with, look at the projects around your own place, government or private owned, which have been abandoned halfway through. No matter what country you're in, millions of dollars along with the corresponding material resources are wasted because of poor planning.

In case of organizations, they all have their stories of how, in anticipation of orders from marketing, materials were procured and processes were set up and the order never materialized. We note how organizations did forward-buying to stock materials or produced to stock finished products but the market never picked up. Management failed to anticipate technological change, competition, or changed customer preferences and ended up with huge stocks of unsold products--materials procured for development activities but never used.

Carrying huge inventories, items in the inventory which become slow moving or obsolete, and items that lose their shelf life all lock up working capital and even turn into severe losses when these items must be scrapped.

Many businesses have closed down owing to the above reasons Every organization will have the same story of finger pointing: it was management's decision, it was marketing's requirement, etc.

1.2) Over design:

This is the first type of wastage that is manifested at the creation stage of a product. Every product that is over designed is a waste. This is a hidden waste and is the highest form of waste.

This form of waste is best detected when we do value analysis and value engineering of the product. What is interesting to note is that, we claim proudly the savings we make after a value analysis and value engineering activity, i.e. revised specifications of input materials to lower levels or materials of lesser cost. But if we look back in retrospect at how long the product carried the unnecessary 'fat' we can realize the loss incurred. As the customer pays for the overdesign, which he will do so as long as gets an alternate choice, the loss is not evident. **But the point for consideration for us is the extra material used and this is the material waste we want to avoid.**

Imagine, those organizations that do not do VE or VA after the initial product development. Let us a check out an example of an overdesigned plastic product weighing 500 gms, the weight of which was reduced by 5% after a value analysis activity. The material saved on 1 million pcs works out to 25 mt! Let us say, 1000 organizations in this industry are manufacturing a similar product, and they also achieve same level of material consumption, the total savings will be 25,000 mt! Imagine the multiplying factor of similar plastic material savings in various industries at a global level.

'OBESE PRODUCTS'

The point I am trying to bring out is that value analysis or value engineering is not a specialist's job. It is best done when a group of employees from various functions such as materials, engineering, manufacturing, design, and quality control as a team analyze and work the 'fat'(the unwanted materials used in the product) out of the 'obese' product.

If looked at, most of the products we use may fall in the 'Obese' product category. There is tremendous potential in removing the unwanted 'fat' out of our products. When this is done in the case of human beings, we use less energy when we reduce the excess fat. Similarly our entire business will automatically use less energy and resources in their manufacturing, packing, transportation usage and disposal.

The MRD is a 24 x 7 value engineering, value analysis team. They can institute all controls to material utilization and consumption right at the conception and inception stage itself. This will save millions of tons of material resources of various types in every industry before they realize the excess material being used. Many will never become aware of it. Time is running out.

1.3) Inadequate manufacturing process:

 The next major contributor to wastage of material is the inprocess wastage. Large corporations and multinational organizations being technologically strong may have process capabilities in place such that they might not have abnormal material wastage. This need not be true of all MNCs across the globe. A MNC in USA or Europe may not necessarily have the same standards in materials consumption and wastage as in China and India where the material resources are cheaper. And even if MNCs have control over their material resource consumption, there will always be scope for continuous improvements. But this is not true for certain other organizations in various industries.

In our present set-up, process wastage is left out as a manufacturing problem but they need to solve it. They, too, blame it on designing, technology and other engineering aspects as an excuse to focus on production rather than the saving of the wastages.

As long as the process wastage is added onto the cost, the management is not worried because the customer pays for it. And as long as the materials are available, nobody is bothered about the wastage right under their noses!

And how many organizations verify the actual wastage against theoretical or initial calculations is also left to be seen. We are not even concerned about the material resources being wasted because of process incapability or lack of in-process controls.

Now process incapability can occur because of improper technology, machinery that is not capable of producing to specifications, non-standard materials specifications, inadequate specifications and design of the product, type or quality of materials used, improper facilities at the plant such as inadequate lighting, frequent power outages, frequent changes of product line, rush orders and so on. In all these aspects, manufacturing is at the receiving end. Sales will chase them for product delivery and manufacturing will keep production going to meet monthly targets.

Under MRD, material process wastage on any account will not be just a manufacturing problem. Every aspect of the process capability will be considered by MRD, be it engineering, materials, product design, plant facilities, manufacturing controls or technology as they are one team and will work together to minimize wastage and set process controls at 6-sigma levels.

1.4) Transportation, storage and handling losses:

In the developed countries and where standard warehousing and logistics services operate this might not be a big issue. But in the developing and under-developed countries, inadequate transportation, storage and handling systems contribute to a lot of transit and poor storage wastages. The essential responsibilities of transportation are to ensure that wastage of all materials is avoided, be it raw, semi or finished goods during handling, storage and transportation.

The above is a general area of focus for the MRD department to deliver the expectations in terms of conservation of material resources.

INDUSTRY:

Now, let us see how MRD can conserve material resources from an industrial point of view.

An industry stands for a collective group of organizations engaged in a similar type of business activities. Therefore, if one organization does an improvement activity in terms of material resources conservation or environmental protection activity, if the entire industry emulates them, imagine the impact the entire industry could create.

Let's consider the manufacture of toys out of virgin plastic material, the basic raw material of which is resin. Resin comes from the petroleum industry for which crude oil is the raw material. Crude oil, as we know, is a fast depleting natural resource and the saving of oil consumption can prolong the stocks for a longer time and give us enough time to develop an alternate to crude oil.

Now, let us say, the MRD in every organization in this industry works on conservation of material resource and each one of them develop their own idea of reducing consumption of resin, wastage, and even recycling the wastage for re-use of their different types of product. Collectively, the MRD in each organization has consciously worked to bring down the consumption and wastage of resin in their industry. This is one example as to how MRD can work toward materials conservation.

2) Impact on Environment:

Today, the business world is considered to be responsible-in-chief for the environment's degradation. After material resource depletion, the other equally important concern is the environmental pollution by our manufacturing industries which has led to ozone layer depletion and climate change wreaking adverse effect on our earth. Fortunately, the world has become conscious of this major issue and many initiatives have been taken at various national and international levels to reduce the impact on our environment.

Besides manufacturing, the other 'crime doers', so to speak, are the transportation or the logistics industry through inefficient fuel efficiency of the transportation vehicles that emit CO_2 gases. The logistics industry is dependent on the automobile industry for providing it with such vehicles. Therefore, as mentioned earlier, the interdependency of industry on the other is again evident. Therefore, if there are MRDs in the automobile industry, the MRD team will work toward providing the logistics industry with fuel efficient, low carbon emission vehicles.

MRD will contribute to the reduction in the impact of environment through direct focus on the manufacturing process as we saw earlier. The bringing of manufacturing, materials, engineering and sales under one head results in focusing and creating a combined intellectual effort to reduce and avoid pollution which is a crying need today.

Organization:

We cannot estimate how many industries and how many organizations are actually involved in reducing environmental impact. We hear about large corporations and multinational companies working on such initiatives but there are thousands of smaller organizations who are not organized and have no clue what has to be done.

Ignorance apart, even some organized sectors are not bothering to work on this aspect. The MRD concept and the responsibilities will be an automatic way of making every industry work in this direction. After all, under the MRD concept, we are trying to develop professionals directed and motivated to work to this end.

MRD AND ISO 9001 CERTIFIED ORGANIZATIONS:

Today, we regard any ISO 9001 certified organizations as one with internationally accepted management systems and procedures. This makes it convenient for all dealings between organizations, nationally or internationally, to work under smooth business practices. The business world has seen the benefit of the ISO certification.

Similarly, under the MRD concept, when one MRD organization deals with the other, they will be dealing with their respective MRD departments whose sense of responsibility and understanding will be mutual. This will make the deliverables in business smoother and faster. That is why the supplier and customer relationship management assumes greater importance under the MRD concept. We mentioned earlier that the product of an organization or industry is the input of the other organizations and industries.

This creates a direct or an indirect link between them. When there is a strong supplier-customer relationship between three firms, the supplier, the user and the user's customer and if this is replicated with successful suppliers on the upstream and customers in the downstream, and if all these organizations are MRD organizations, ***then we have a 'common business thinking and practicing' MRD business chain link.***

As mentioned above, supplier relationship and customer relationship form a very integral part of the MRD concept. We will therefore deal with this topic in detail in the next chapter and see how a good supplier relationship takes care of the customer relationship and customer satisfaction, leading to increase in business and profitability which I call the 'Profitability Continuum'.

This we will see in the next chapter.

CHAPTER 6

Supplier & Customer Relationship Management

WE ARE NOW done with creating an MRD-model organization.

To sum up, we have defined the Tangible and Intangible materials resources groups which is the base of MRD concept, re-organized the framework along these lines with the newly created MRD department, marketing, finance and HRD reporting to the CEO. We then looked at some of the changed roles of marketing and finance, the roles and responsibilities of MRD department and the MRD head.

All this was done with an aim to:

One: Focus on material resources, its optimum utility by avoiding environmental degradation.

Two: focus on material resources which will enable its better utilization and productivity, thereby improving the profitability of the organization.

Three: re-organize organizational structure, with a focus on material resources and the utilization group brought together under one head, helps to break down the supply chain within the organization into one unit. This, in turn, improves the business process for greater efficiency and effectiveness, further improving the profitability and the organization's competitiveness.

Now, we look at the business aspect of the organization externally.

RELATIONSHIP WITH SUPPLIERS AND CUSTOMERS:

The MRD department was created based on tangible materials resources. We have considered procurement and sales which handle these material resources as part of the MRD department by handling the resources in two different forms, that is, incoming materials of the organization and the outgoing materials in the form of finished products.

This entire handbook is designed at a simple level so that even the novice business owner can understand each concept. Let us review: the sources from which the material resources come, (the suppliers), and where, after process, they go to, (the customers), are two of the most vital aspects of business for every organization, be it in manufacturing or trading. If the suppliers do not supply and the customers do not buy, an organization very hastily becomes defunct. It will cease to exist unless these two aspects are revived and there is a continuous flow of the materials on site: the incoming and the outgoing. Therefore, the suppliers and customers become a very integral part of the MRD concept.

If an organization works on the MRD concept and has their suppliers and customers also working on the same concept, we will have smooth flow of material resources between these organizations which can be known as the MRD chain.

As you know, in the supply chain management, we refer to the *upstream* as all those input materials moving into the organization from the suppliers for manufacture and *downstream* represents the flow of manufactured products out of the organization to the customers. Under MRD, we saw how we reorganized the internal supply chain model to now form a totally integrated department by itself. Therefore, we no more have a supply chain within the organization that links each process with the other to complete the manufacturing activity and dispatch to the customer, but an integrated business process that takes care of all these activities as one unit.

The suppliers and the customers will now find it very convenient to deal with the MRD department as, instead of interacting with various business process units of the organization such as procurement, quality, manufacturing, engineering separately, they need to deal with only one integrated unit, thus making their transactions of technical or commercial aspects clearer and faster, improving the business process and lead times drastically.

Under our present organizational set up, although the importance of suppliers and customers have grown, the above mentioned transactional problem is one of the main issues faced by the suppliers and customers. They are required to deal, that is, to interact with different business process functions to finalize an order within the organization.

What happens now is that the design, quality and engineering give written specs and the procurement department and supplier have to wait to interact with these departments separately and seek clarification and approval from them and their respective bosses to understand the needs of the organization as well as express their capability or limitations to the organization to make an offer and supply.

Under the MRD concept, it will be one team consisting of the various business units that will be dealing with the supplier or the customer.

This is possible because, as seen earlier under MRD, each function has supporting responsibilities for the other function. Thus, one such responsibility of design, manufacturing, or quality engineer will be to finalize technically correct purchase orders with the supplier.

Similarly, when customers approach an organization for an offer, they often have to wait endlessly to get an offer till such time as all the above-mentioned functions have understood and finalized their input to the marketing department for the quotation to the customers. The customers face similar problems when they look out for after-sales services and product failure problems.

But the most important aspect to understand is that, unlike the way the business processes within an organization are carried out, dealing with the outside agencies like the supplier and the customer is not the same. It requires much more understanding, diplomacy and relationship building to ensure that the transactions with them go smoothly and are developed on a long term basis.

The jobs of procurement and marketing & sales, in this context, is a tough one. They have to play the balancing act of satisfying the needs of these outside agencies as well as meeting the requirements of the internal functions to protect the interests of the organization. This means a lot for the organization's business success as well as its image outside in the industry and business world. The most basic requirement for achieving success is a good Supplier Relationship Management (SRM) and Customer Relationship Management (CRM).

Any problem in the flow of goods, from the upstream or toward the downstream, can adversely affect the performance of the organization. Hence, over the years, especially when TQM became a business model, the importance of maintaining the flow of goods from the upside and toward the downside, has been attributed to the **relationship** the organization builds and maintains with these two groups - the suppliers and the customers.

Therefore, it is important to understand and integrate these two vital business relationships: the SRM and CRM within the organization. As seen earlier, these two groups which are essentially and directly connected with material resources are an integral part of the MRD concept. We must focus on making the relationship with these two groups very efficient and seamless in order to make the MRD concept successful. These relationships must be considered as very vital **life-line support** for the organization.

While all organizations give great importance to the management of the customer relationship, (the Customer Relationship Management – CRM), the same importance is not given for Supplier Relationship Management – SRM, which is still a growing terminology. We will see later in this chapter, how by focusing more on SRM, CRM improves automatically, leading to more business and profitability which I call the '**Profitability Continuum**'.

Organizations accept that the 'Customer is the King', at least in a buyer's market, and the top management goes all-out to please the customers. However, the suppliers, who actually fund the organization by giving them materials on credit, make materials available to the organization to manufacture their products, are often taken for granted.

Now, let me give you some background aspects on the supplier and customer relationship from an organizational and marketing point of view.

SUPPLIER RELATIONSHIP MANAGEMENT (SRM)

Today, procurement functions in the supply chain with important roles within and outside the organization. It interacts within the organization with marketing/sales, design/engineering and operations/ manufacturing to consolidate their requirements and source the same from the vast number of suppliers in the market. The success and failure of the purchasing function is determined by these suppliers.

A failure in the performance of the suppliers can spell doom for the organization and good performance keeps the organization in business, supports growth and innovation, and helps improve profits through savings in materials cost. How does this happen?

There was a time when organizations, except for general supply items, manufactured all their items related to its products directly or indirectly. Hence, they were self sufficient in all their requirements and were not dependent on outside sources.

As time passed, the cost of materials, labor and overhead started rising and the broadcast for quantity of products, with growing demand in the market, also increased. Added to this, the cost of capital also increased and it became difficult for manufacturers to maintain an elaborate facility for all their requirements. Moreover, the ever-increasing demand in the market required the manufacturers to concentrate on increasing production of their main product and they utilized most resources for this purpose. They were also pressured to improve productivity and spend money prudently, keeping in mind the increasing capital cost and the importance of maintaining their working capital.

I mentioned the point earlier in this book, that as growth, development and modernization in the industry developed, many specialized and common requirements for manufacturers such as fabrication, machine workshop, painting works, smelting and casting works, packing material, etc. started emerging. This made it convenient for the manufacturers to specify and off load such jobs to outside sources. Moreover, this worked out cheaper as the outside source could distribute its cost over a larger quantity of similar products it manufactured for others. This process developed and led to outsourcing.

Outsourcing helped the manufacturers to first off-load their non-critical jobs to outside sources. Next came those jobs that were specialized in nature and in-house manufacturing required large investment. The emergence of vendors ready to invest in specialized technology solved this problem. By outsourcing, the manufacturers could concentrate on their main product manufacturing, productivity and quality.

Over a period of time, farming out or the outsourcing practice became very cost effective and today, organizations all over the world outsource most of their requirement in terms of materials – processed, unprocessed, semi-processed, components and parts, services, job works, MROs etc. This brought the suppliers to the fore in business and has made them an essential part of our business today and we are heavily reliant on them for running our businesses.

ROLE OF SUPPLIERS

An organization develops suppliers to meet their quantity, quality and delivery requirements and they enter into contractual understandings specifying price and other terms of business with the supplier. As large numbers of items are outsourced and the quantities required are also large, the organizations have to have a large network of suppliers to meet this demand. This led to recognition of purchasing as the management element that developed and managed the suppliers, warehoused the materials received from the suppliers and regulated the inventories in coordination with purchasing. Transportation arranged collection and delivery of the material from the suppliers and clearance of material from the ports. This coordinated activity developed into materials management.

Increasing market volumes, stiff market competition, demand by customers for quality products, delivery on time and better pricing brought home the realization of the need to coordinate the elements involved, within and without the organization in the supply of the products to the customer.

Hence, such elements that were involved in getting orders from the customers, material planning, production planning, materials procurement and supplier management, manufacturing, quality control, engineering, R&D, storage and issue of materials and products and delivery of the products to the customer were aligned to coordinate, expedite, de-bottle neck problems in this process, and work to make timely supply of quality products to the customer base which was called the supply chain.

One major component in the supply chain was the outside agency that purchasing handled and that was the large set of suppliers that delivered almost all the material and service requirements of the organization. The management of this large group of suppliers and coordinating its functions with the internal elements for converting the materials into customer orders in the supply chain right up to the customer's customer came to be called the SUPPLY CHAIN MANAGEMENT (SCM).

As mentioned earlier, the MM function looks after coordinating the purchasing, warehousing and transport activities to service its internal customer –manufacturing. SCM includes the activities of marketing and manufacturing in its supply chain activities and aligns the supplier's performance to the organizations' internal requirements right up to the final customer.

As almost all requirements of organizations today in terms of material, components, job work and other services are outsourced, they are heavily reliant on their vast number of suppliers for timely supply of the materials. A failure on the part of one supplier in terms of delivery, quality or any breakdown at its facility must be covered by the other suppliers to ensure uninterrupted supply for the organization. Continuous follow-up with the suppliers through correspondence, meetings and visits, along with training for the suppliers on quality improvement and technical knowledge are essential to ensure continuous supply and improvement in the delivered products.

In short, keeping due vigilance on the market situation and the vast number of organizations' suppliers, keeping them motivated, improving their performance and making them work like one big team is a herculean task purchasing performs in the supply chain. This activity, as mentioned earlier, is the lifeline of the organization, as it is this vital interaction between the purchasing and the suppliers that ensure continuous supply and keep the manufacturing running. Any failure on this front can bring organizations to a grinding halt.

An uninterrupted performance from the suppliers is the result of a great coordinated team effort between purchasing and the suppliers. There is a great sense of understanding regarding each other's duties, responsibilities and obligations to be successful. The success or failure of this interaction is based on the relationship purchasing builds with each supplier. This vital relationship is simply called the supplier relationship.

SUPPLIER RELATIONSHIP MANAGEMENT (SRM):

We can define the supplier relationship as an attractive force between the supplier and the organization to work together to achieve each other's business goals. This attractive force is held together by mutual respect, trust and realization of each other's goals.

A failure in any of these aspects sours and may even break the relationship. Relationship builds over a period of time, which leads to the vendors investing more in the organization, developing into strategic relationships and becoming business partners. The management of this relationship with each of its suppliers into a fruitful win-win business result for the organization and the suppliers is obviously referred to as the supplier relationship management.

Managing supplier relationship is a science as well as an art. The art is the organization's style and attitude in dealing with the suppliers and the science refers to the various materials management techniques used to achieve the business goals. A good attitude toward suppliers wins their acceptance to put the techniques into practice. Only attitude or only technique never yields the desired results. Hence, it is very important to combine the two judiciously to enjoy the best results.

As from an MRD point of view, the MRD department's interaction with the suppliers becomes a joint responsibility of various business functions now in the MRD department.

Therefore, it is important for us to go into the details of this relationship. We will first look into the scientific aspect of the supplier relationship management and later into its similarity to an art.

A good supplier relationship management requires some basics or foundation. The first one is:

KNOW YOUR PLAYING FIELD:

Every organization by virtue of its presence and interaction in the market creates for itself an image and reputation in the market.

It is very important for an organization to know where it stands in the market. One cannot bulldoze ones way into the market in terms of supplier development, retainment and performance from the suppliers. The organization has only so much power to dictate terms to the suppliers in regard to the **IMAGE AND REPUTATION of** the organization in the market. Therefore, a blue chip organization and a failing organization will have a different say in the market.

A very important aspect to remember is that the supplier is a very shrewd and knowledgeable businessperson wanting to put money into an organization where the money is safe. He can get a steady business and good or reasonable return for his investment. He is not into charity. Just as a common man studies and decides after careful evaluation of an organization's performance to invest in its shares, the supplier, too, evaluates the performance of the organization before investing his money into the organization he wishes to supply. This is reflected by the image and reputation the organization has created for itself in carrying out its business.

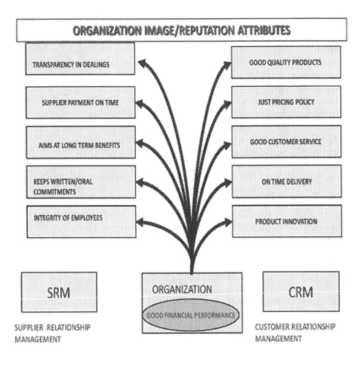

Along with the financial performance, the supplier fraternity judges the image of an organization on aspects that deal with typical supplier's business interests.

It looks for whether the organization:

Honors written and oral commitments:

This is a very vital concern for the suppliers. There cannot be a greater breach of trust than an organization failing to live up to its written or oral commitments with its suppliers. Once a purchase order is placed or a contract signed with a supplier, or oral assurances and agreement reached, the organization must ensure that it meets all requirements on its part and does not change its mind mid-way, leading to losses for the supplier and having to go into litigation to recover losses.

There cannot be a more damaging loss of reputation for an organization than a supplier taking it to court for having failed to meet its commitment. More damages follow as word quickly spreads among the supplier fraternity of such cases and they become wary of doing business with the organization. This can directly impact relationship with existing suppliers and their supplies to the organization.

Therefore, it is the responsibility of all elements in the supply chain of an organization to plan accurately before committing to the suppliers. If the organization is stepping out of its commitment by no fault of the supplier, it must reasonably compensate the supplier if it is not being done under a contract. Most suppliers of low value supplies do not have signed agreements to offer supplies to the organization. Nor are such suppliers conversant with the legalities of business. They just rely on the purchase order and make supply based on trust. Unless proved otherwise, in my twenty-five years of experience, by and large, I have found suppliers to the organizations with which I worked trustworthy.

You can measure the number of litigation cases filed by the suppliers against the organization or written/oral complaints submitted by the suppliers to the management as a gauge of the organization's trustworthiness with their suppliers.

Looks for Long term or Short term benefits:

A good attitude of the organization towards its suppliers is reflected if it works with them on a long term basis. If the attitude is to use the supplier for short term benefits and then change them (use-and discard attitude), the suppliers do not show confidence in dealing with the organization and there will be no commitment. They, too, will do short term business and leave the organization as soon as another good business opportunity comes along. Reputed suppliers in the market do not approach such organizations, thereby depriving the organization of quality suppliers.

You can easily measure this by the organization's turnover of suppliers during a typical year. It reflects your 'supplier jumping' or the supplier leaving you.

Makes Supplier payments on time:

The credit worthiness of an organization is known by its on-time payment to its suppliers. It's a known fact that the organization releases payment to its suppliers only after making its statutory payments. A reasonable delay from the stated payment term may be acceptable but a deliberate delay with a view to utilize the supplier's money for doing business reflects poorly on the organization.

Delayed payment on account of poor funds also reflects negatively on the financial status of the organization and keeps away new suppliers from doing business. Existing suppliers also find the next best opportunity to cease doing business with the organization. One should remember that in case of delayed payment, the organization has to pay higher prices charged by the suppliers as there will be lesser suppliers willing to supply. Also, the existing suppliers may join together to quote higher prices. This eventually leads to higher product cost and the organization becomes out-priced in the market resulting in dwindling market share.

This can be measured by the number of creditors the organization has on their books for long periods. Figure the average number of delay in days against credit terms as well as comparing it with the number of day's debtors as against creditors. This will reflect whether there is deliberate delay in releasing the suppliers' funds.

Shows transparency in its dealings:

The suppliers appreciate organizations that are transparent in their dealings with their suppliers. They should offer a reasonable opportunity for them to negotiate for orders, state reasons in case orders are not placed, explain the organization's policies and share with them the organization's business plans and achievements, its problems and opportunities. It also helps to schedule open house supplier meetings. These are some good examples of transparency.

Transparency will be greatly appreciated by the suppliers and they will prefer to work for such organizations rather than those that are not open and where the management is not concerned about the suppliers and is unapproachable.

To understand this, check whether the organization has an open door policy for the suppliers and whether the head of the purchasing or materials management meet with all the suppliers on a regular basis.

Employees with integrity:

Integrity means being honest and fair. Every employee that deals with the supplier must exhibit this quality in his or her dealings with him or her. Dishonest and unfair employees seriously tarnish the image and reputation of an organization. Purchasing professionals must not play one supplier against the other or give wrong promises and projections with a view to rope in the supplier for business. Technical people who deal with the supplier should be fair in their technical specifications and requirements and have uniform consideration for all concerned suppliers.

Similarly, payment to suppliers should not be based on favor or bias. Employees represent the organization and their character reflects its image and reputation in the marketplace. Employees with high integrity can bring in more suppliers and the opposite can make existing suppliers leave the organization. Unscrupulous suppliers and employees, when they combine, do unethical business and make the organization a haven for corruption. No need to add that such organizations become infamous in the market and do not survive for long.

The best measure of this is the internal and external audit reports of the organization which can give a fair idea of the commercial and technical transactions and judge the integrity of the employees as well as uncover any unethical practices. An audit of the external environment of the organization with the organization's customers, suppliers, dealers, and traders can also reveal the organization's reputation represented by its employees.

These are a few major aspects important to reflect the image and reputation of the organization. There may be more. What is important is that suppliers dealing with the organization carry their opinion, based on their dealings with the organization in the supplier fraternity, in the market, and in certain cases even to the general public. Therefore, whatever an organization does, it must be to enhance its reputation and image in the market, not tarnish it.

All this has a direct impact on the customers of the organization because the customers will also judge your image and reputation in the market based on the ways you deal with the suppliers. Needless to add the shareholders and the share market also keep a close watch on this aspect.

CUSTOMER RELATIONSHIP MANAGEMENT (CRM):

We have viewed the reputation and image of the organization from a supplier point of view. Now, let us look at the reputation of an organization from a customer point of view, which is what marketing strives to enhance and is called the Customer Relationship Management (CRM).

We will also try to understand how these two relationships complement each other and affect the image and reputation of the organization. 'As you sow, so do you reap' is a saying that fits this description perfectly because if you do not maintain a good supplier relationship, it reflects a poor image and reputation of your organization in the marketplace. For the customers, you become their suppliers. When they do supplier evaluation, they will definitely not deal with a supplier who has a bad reputation in the market.

CUSTOMER'S EXPECTATIONS:

Good Quality Products:

Customer seek the worth for their monies in the products they buy. Good quality stands for 'fitness for purpose or use' and if the product meets this end, the product sells in the market with the image and reputation of the organization. If the products sold are of substandard quality and not consistent in quality, the corollary is that the organization cannot motivate its suppliers to give them high quality material when they are themselves supplying substandard products in the market.

However, if the organization presents themselves as quality product suppliers themselves, then it will have the same response and performance from their suppliers. They will attract good quality suppliers.

A Just Pricing Policy:

Markets are very dynamic in terms of price, which is reflected by the prevailing demand and supply conditions. The organization has the choice to be just in its pricing policy or make hay while the sun shines by demanding higher prices when it can do so.

The corollary is that the suppliers too will have a similar attitude toward their supply to the organization. Then the organization will have unsteady prices of their input materials, making it difficult for them to have a pricing strategy.

Good Customer Service:

Service before, during, and after sales is the expectation of every customer. This reflects sincerity in your dealing with the customer and confidence in your product and your regard for a long-term relationship with the customer.

The suppliers also expect you to hold their hand at the time of supplier development, trial orders and in their growth toward being a reliable supplier for the organization through proper introduction to the organization's activities and requirements. The organization must identify what business it can do best with the chosen supplier, and then guide and train them to meet the requirements and help them grow with the organization.

The corollary is that, if you have good customer service, the suppliers know what they can expect from you and will stay with you for a long-term relationship.

On-Time Delivery:

Every customer expects its orders to be serviced on time. Delayed deliveries not only delay further activities of the customer but can also result in financial loss for the customer. A market reputation of delayed deliveries can affect the organization and result in a severe loss of business opportunity.

The corollary is that the suppliers, too, may not consider making timely deliveries to the organization as important. This mentality must be altered.

Product innovation:

If the organization does not improve or innovate its products, its performance will remain static or, over a period, slide downward. This means that the customers will remain with the organization for some time but, later, may go for the latest technology products elsewhere.

The corollary is that your suppliers will also not find any reason to invest in quality and design improvement in the products they supply to the organization. The sad part is that the more dynamic suppliers who look for creativity, business challenges, and growth may leave the organization for business elsewhere.

We can see that the customer relationship management (CRM) is a mirror image of supplier relationship management (SRM). The organization, as a supplier to its customer cannot expect any better from its suppliers than what it gives to its own customers.

'As you sow, so do you reap' is an old saying that exemplifies the above corollaries.

Therefore, reputed organizations all over the world have at their back end a well-established supplier base that services them the way they service their customers. The secret to this is a good reputation and image in the market, which creates a level playing field for the organization to work with the suppliers in the market on equal terms or by positioning themselves higher, therefore being in a position to lead and develop a good supplier relationship management (SRM). Those who lack in their image and reputation must work seriously on improving the aspects mentioned above to enable an improved image and reputation in the market.

In other words, a good **CRM** (customer relationship management) can help in good **SRM** (supplier relationship management).

THE PROFITABILITY CONTINUUM:

Having established the commonality between the supplier relationship management and the customer relationship management and its interrelationships, let me now make you aware of a very important fact that arises from this understanding.

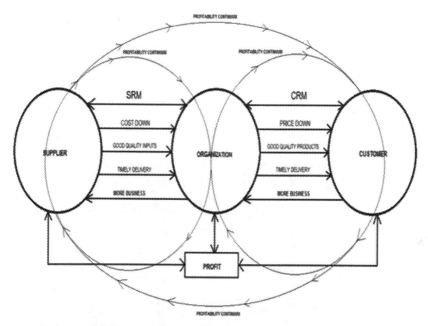

PROFITABILITY CONTINUUM: Focus on Supplier Relationship Management (SRM) reflects on the organization's performance impacting the Customer Relationship Management (CRM) which returns more business and profit continuously for all three-organization, supplier and customer

In the above diagram, you will note the circle on the left, SRM, which stands for the suppliers and the organization's relationship with them.

When the relationship is good, it results in and gives the organization: 'Cost down' over a period of time owing to assured business, learning curve, and other factors. 'Better Quality' arising out of the close relationship leads to a better understanding of each other's technical needs and supplier training, and 'timely delivery' arises out of the close interaction on quantity requirement and correct scheduling of deliveries from the suppliers.

Now let us look at the CRM in the circle on the right side which stands for customer and the organization's relationship with them.

When the SRM is good we saw that the organization gets –cost cuts, better quality and timely delivery.

Now what does this result in for the organization?

It results in the organization making products for its customers as scheduled because of timely delivery for the suppliers and fine quality. The cost savings on the input materials worked out with the suppliers help the organization to reduce their prices to their customers.

When you deliver on-time, good quality products with better prices for your customers, it results in developing better relationships with the customers automatically and they respond with 'Increased volume of business' for the organization!

When you get higher volume of business, you will first share with your regular suppliers who, in turn, will respond with better pricing for the increased volume of business. This helps you, thus, to consider better pricing for your customers. This should happen regularly and continuously over a long period of time with the same set of suppliers and customers or and a new set of suppliers and customers. This is what I call the 'Profitability Continuum'. This is a result of the focus on the SRM that has led to a good CRM automatically. You can thereafter do more things to satisfy your customer further and enhance your customer relationship.

THE PERFECT TEN:

As in gymnastics, when an athlete gets ten points out of ten, it is called a perfect ten. (You may recollect Nadia Comaneci scoring for the first time in the history of Olympics a perfect '10' score in a gymnastic event). Now we will talk about something similar for our organizations- attempting to achieve a perfect ten score in SRM and CRM!

The idea behind this is to ensure that you balance your relationship in five major criteria with your suppliers as well as your customers with two points for each criterion.

SUPPLIER CRITERIA	CUSTOMER CRITERIA
1) QUALITY RECEIVED	1) QUALITY DELIVERED
2) ON TIME DELIVERY RECEIVED	2) ON TIME DELIVERY MADE
3) ON TIME PAYMENTS MADE	3)ON TIME PAYMENTS RECEIVED
4) PRICE ACCEPTABILITY	4) PRICE ACCEPTABILITY
5) SERVICE RESPONSE RECEIVED	5)SERVICE RESPONSE GIVEN

I will explain each of the criteria:

1) QUALITY RECEIVED: This reflects the in-coming materials received from your suppliers—its acceptance versus rejection percentage.

Similarly, what you deliver to your customer can be calculated on a percentage basis.

2) ON-TIME DELIVERY RECEIVED: This refers to the delivery dates of the supplier as per order based on ex-works shipment basis or door delivered basis.

Similarly, you can work out the delivery performance of your organization to the customer.

3) ON-TIME PAYMENTS MADE: This refers to the payments to the suppliers for the supplies made and its deviation from the actual date of payment as per payment terms to work out the delay.

Similarly, you can calculate the date of payment made by the customer as per payment terms and the deviation from the due date.

4) PRICE ACCEPTABILITY: You will have a price agreed upon with the supplier. But you must be able to establish whether that is the right price. This you can do on the basis of two factors. One: estimate your own pricing based on your calculations and, two: find out market price. You will be able to establish the 'lesser than' or 'greater than' price factor and give marks accordingly.

Similarly, you can establish your prices to your customers comparing them with the market prices and give marks accordingly.

5) SERVICE RESPONSE RECEIVED: This refers to how the supplier responds to your request for after-sales services and response to improve quality and price reduction activities as well as meet the 'green' requirement.

Similarly, the response is important in terms of time taken to respond to a call from customer for after-sales service and number of days to settle the matter as per fixed norms. This also helps determine your grade.

For each of the above criteria, you must work out your marks out of two marks for each. If you can get a perfect ten on either side, it reflects well. If it is a perfect ten on both sides, it's simply GREAT!

Other than the above, we can have additional criteria on both sides and apportion the marks within the ten marks to be able to look at the magic figure of a perfect ten.

For the 'Perfect Ten' idea it is helpful to understand that the SRM and CRM are mirror images and one reflects the other in the way we handle it.

Now, one more important aspect I would like to share with you is that you must bear in mind that each one of you will be in an organization that will be in a different phase of business growth and therefore all business management techniques will have applicability depending upon your particular business phase, which I will now address.

UNDERSTAND YOUR BUSINESS SITUATION:

The business situations for all organizations are not similar. They vary based on industry, economic and business environment —whether it's local and global, market demand and supply and, most important, the performance of the organization against all these conditions and challenges.

The other major aspects include the organization's own growth plan and business strategy. In keeping with the market forces or otherwise (bold ventures), the organization can choose to grow at multiple rates through enhancement of its manufacturing capacity, diversification into newer fields of business, or a choice to grow at a steady pace with short and long term plans and strategies. In either of these cases, the organization can either succeed or fail.

Success means that the organization meets its multiple growth or steady growth plans. But a failure in meeting their respective growth plans converts such an organization into a 'failing organization' i.e. it begins to stagnate, lose market share, struggles to make profit and is on its way toward losses.

It is very important to note that organizations find themselves in each of the business situations out of choice, poor management, or market conditions. These situations are not static, as these very factors can propel them into any of the business situations. Business is dynamic and, just as a seismograph monitors continuously the 'happenings' under the earth's crust, management must be vigilant to every aspect in this constantly changing world of business environment and thus guide its management efforts to remain on the course it has chosen for itself.

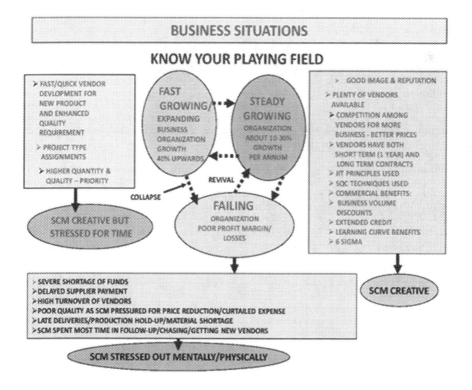

BUSINESS SITUATION is dynamic. A 'Fast Growing' organization can become a 'Steady' or a 'Failing' organization and vice versa. Supply Chain Management (SCM) techniques must be used suitably.

Any organization, in each of the above 'business situations' requires different management techniques for its maintenance, growth or revival. Similarly, SRM also varies in each of the three types of business situations. Based on the above, we can classify these three types of business situations as:

1) Fast growing organization
2) Steadily growing or static organization
3) Failing organization

It is important to understand how SRM works in each of the above general business situations because management techniques do not require, so to speak, 'a common pill for all ailments.' Management vows are reached or successes achieved based on selective use of the management techniques.

Similarly, organizations must understand each unique business situation and choose the appropriate MM, SCM and SRM techniques.

Therefore, a fast growing organization's needs will be to enhance quantity to meet its ever-increasing demand for material and, as such, supplier development will be its priority.

For a steady growing organization, to consolidate its position in the market, cost reduction, quality improvement, product innovation, supplier training, on-time deliveries, and long term agreements will become the priorities.

Whereas, for a failing organization, it must 1) hold on to its existing suppliers (suppliers tend to leave failing organizations as the first impact is delayed payments to the suppliers), 2) follow up deliveries (suppliers deliberately delay supplies to keep their money locked to a minimum), it must 3) use value engineering and value analysis to look for alternate material, 4) and it must make an effort at cost reduction to improve material to sales ratio or reduced product price in the market.

In this type of business, if the suppliers are handled properly, they can go a long way toward helping the organization during its crisis period (note that the suppliers are a financer to the organization) and be a rescuer for the organization enabling it to get out of the red. It's all based on the relationship the organization has developed with the suppliers.

The business situations mentioned above are very 'liquid' in the sense that one wrong move or one change in the business environment can seriously affect the fortunes of organizations overnight and it's the suppliers that the organizations can fall back on during such difficult times. This will depend upon how the organization has nurtured its relationship with the suppliers over the years. This will help us understand the importance of 'Supplier Relationship Management' for perpetuity.

FAST-GROWING ORGANIZATION:

In this type of business situation, organizations are on the fast growth track.

This can be categorized into two types of organizations. One is new to business and, therefore, during the initial years, works very fast to reach its desired level of break-even sales and then surpass it to meet budget targets. Such organizations are those that have just taken off after project completion.

The second relates to those businesses which are already established and doing very well. They might be riding on the back of very good demand in the market and commanding a good market share which makes the organization grow at a very robust pace, say, 40 to 50% annually or even doubling the sales annually.

The MM, SCM and SRM here are focused on meeting the annual manufacturing targets. There is great demand in terms of volume of material to meet higher production for which reason the priority is developing new suppliers to meet the increasing demand.

A second important criterion is to follow up with suppliers for timely delivery to meet uninterrupted supply because the consumption rate of material will be very high. Hence, a focus on contractual obligations with the suppliers for timely delivery and close follow-up is the priority. Price may not be of the highest concern as the organization is in the driver's seat in the market and therefore commands a fair price for its product and has a good margin of profit. It will go in for good quality products and reputed suppliers.

As business is good and it can forecast long-term requirements, it can enter into long term contracts with the suppliers and may even consider investing in the business of certain critical component suppliers, thus developing a business partnership.

The supply chain employees in such an organization devote much of their time in vendor development and follow-up for materials so as to ensure quality. As the organization is growing fast, and if it is able to create a good image and reputation in the eyes of the customer and in the market, then, drawing from the corollary explained earlier, the existing suppliers, as well as new suppliers, will be willing to come onboard and become a link to the organization.

The supplier and organization relations are cordial and this motivates the supplier's willingness to invest more with the growing demands of the organization. In this type of a business, the suppliers must be paid on time to ensure continuous cash availability so the supplier can procure material and supply consistently.

The employees in all departments of an organization may be stressed to meet the high volume continuous increase in demand. However, the morale will be high as they are part of a performing, growing organization and the work involved is very creative as they face new challenges in MM, SCM and SRM in the fast growing phase of the organization. Another motivating factor is the growing business benefits the management shares with the employees.

STEADY GROWING ORGANIZATION:

Globally, most of the organizations fall into this category. They include large, medium and small organizations. These types of organizations have a steady market and the growth potential annually is ruled by market conditions or by choice of the organizations to grow at a steady pace. They work out their plan to increase market share, profit margin, annual turnover, product innovation, business diversification, etc. Such organizations have to work on continuous business improvements in order to survive against market competition. Therefore, they learn and implement both well known and newly developed business practices in terms of technology and management.

Because of the steady nature of business, the principles, practices and techniques of MM, SCM and SRM have the best potential to work in such organizations. Organizations that have understood and implemented this have benefited through huge savings and significant improvement in business performance.

These types of organizations are established in the market and if they have a good image and reputation, it creates a good base upon which to develop supplier relationships. Suppliers offer quality and prompt service as they can expect continuous, long term business and grow with the organization. This leads to competition amongst the suppliers to get business from the organization which, in turn, helps the organization to gain a good base for negotiations and to obtain good prices and terms from the suppliers.

As business grows, discounts on increased volume of business, learning curve, etc. can be obtained. The suppliers, in order to retain business, make concerted efforts to ensure quality and timely supply besides cooperating with the organization to learn and invest if required for continuous improvement that reduces prices and improves quality.

Therefore, for MRD to succeed, a very strong SRM and CRM is a must.

We will now move on to our concluding chapter with a seven-step process for implementing the MRD concept in an organization.

CHAPTER 7

Concluding The MRD Concept

It takes a noble man to plant a seed for a tree that will someday give shade to people he may never meet.

THIS THEN SPEAKS to the role of an MRD head, MRD team, owners and professionals who run businesses and all of us working in the various industries. Every effort to conserve natural resources and protect the environment will help us today as well as the generations to come.

I have put forward a management paradigm which first came to me about ten years back. Since then, I have been working on this thought and have developed it over the years into the present form.

I am neither a professional writer nor a management expert. I have expressed an idea that I feel will be useful for business organizations. This book is a simple and straightforward expression of the same and therefore, devoid of statistics, elaborate theories and case studies. I leave it to those who appreciate this idea, in the form of a concept, to adapt it to their respective businesses in the form I mention in this book or in a modified form that will suit their industry or business. All I wish to gain from such implementation is that it benefitted the industries, businesses, and communities.

As a summary for those wishing to implement the MRD concept, I give below a Seven Step method to enable or ease the implementation.

SEVEN STEPS TO THE MRD CONCEPT IMPLEMENTATION:

STEP 1 – APPOINT THE MRD HEAD

You must first have your MRD head selected. We have seen in detail the qualities and requirements of the MRD head in Chapter 4. Keeping this in mind, you need to find one within your organization or recruit someone from outside. This is a very challenging position and therefore the success of the MRD concept itself rests with the candidate you select for this post.

STEP 2 - The 'As-Is' study:

As in any re-engineering activity, you must first map your organization's current set-up and business process flow.

This is important because we will be making fundamental changes in the organizational set-up as well as the business process flow. You must also identify in the business flow and organizational set-up, key business activities and role players typical to your business so that when we re-organize we do not lose track or focus to ensure that such processes and role players do not get side lined and affect the performance of the organization. On the other hand, while implementing MRD, we will see how the performance of these processes and roles can be enhanced.

To give an example, in the service industry, let us take the example of a hospital. Now in a hospital, the ICU (intensive care unit) becomes the most important treatment process among the various other treatments in process in the hospital for the admitted patients. This is because of the nature of the treatment of the patients in the ICU. They require life support devices, treatment and care to take them out of danger and save their lives. This is also a matter of reputation for the hospital. Hence the key here would be to ensure that the ICU is well maintained from a facility point of view (well painted and clean atmosphere, good lighting, smoothly running air conditioners, curtains, etc.), all medical equipment well maintained for use 24x7, medical and other supplies available all the time. Basically, we are reflecting on the materials resource deployment in the ICU.

Now let us take the example of another important process –surgery. Obviously, here the key personnel are the surgeons. We saw that, in the ICU, besides the medical treatment given, the facilities in the ICU help maintain the patients' vital functions till such time as the medical treatment has had its effects and the person's body starts functioning normally, enabling the patient to be moved to the general care ward.

In case of surgery, the surgeon becomes the focus. For the duration of time that he is in surgery, he should be very well facilitated with all requirements from the right atmosphere in the operation theatre to all other medical facilities required during the course of the surgery. This is vital for a successful operation.

The point I am stressing is how vital for us to know our key business processes and key personnel so that both get the right facility and focus to ensure their performance and the success of the organization's service or products.

In case of an engineering industry, let us consider the example of an organization that designs and manufactures high voltage capacitors for specific applications as per customer needs. Here the most important aspect is the capacitor element. The windings must be made in dust free, temperature controlled conditions besides other technical requirements failing which the capacitor elements can fail. Therefore, the winding room of the capacitor elements in the engineering industry reflects the facilities required for the ICUs in the case of hospitals in the service industry.

Now the capacitors, which are made for specific customer use, require a high level of technical knowledge and experience to design the appropriate product. Therefore, the designers in the design and development department require the necessary facilities such as AutoCAD etc. and a peaceful environment in which to do their creative work. Therefore, the design and development engineer's requirements in the engineering industry reflect the surgeon's requirements in the hospitals!

Having mapped the organizational set-up, business process flow and having identified the vital processes and key personnel, we move to the next step: identifying the tangible and intangible activities.

STEP 3: Identify the Intangible and Tangible activities:

We now move into the MRD concept. We start this by identifying in the business process flow of your organization, all activities that use material resources directly and indirectly for performing their respective activities.

While we have concluded that under the MRD concept, finance, HRD and marketing activities fall under the intangible activities, it is necessary that the organization comes together and does this activity of identifying and segregating the tangible and intangible activities. This is important because, when we move to the next step of re-organizing, the organization's team must know exactly what is happening and why. Any change, if done with the understanding and knowledge of the concerned, becomes easier to implement than a change planned in a conference room among a few executives and then hurried into action. This is more important for business organization, as the earlier a change gets implemented with the least teething problems, so much lesser the learning curve or change cost.

While segregating the tangible and intangible activities, you must follow the basics of the MRD concept that were mentioned in Chapter 2, 3 and 5.

STEP 4- RE-ORGANIZING THE ORGANIZATION:

We now move on to the toughest part of the MRD implementation and that is – re-organizing the organization on the lines of the MRD concept. We will now segregate the business activities of finance, marketing and HRD (the intangible activities in your organization) from the rest of the tangible activities as per the exercise done in the previous step. We will term all the grouped tangible activities as the MRD department. The person heading the MRD department will be referred to as the MRD head.

You must now draw the new organizational chart. You will find that only four business functions report to the CEO. They are finance, marketing, HRD and MRD.

You will also find that all your key processes and personnel will also be under the MRD. Therefore, in the earlier example of engineering and non-engineering firms i.e. a hospital and a manufacturer, you will find that the key process such as ICU or the winding room or in the case of key personnel such as the design engineer or the surgeon, they will all fall under the MRD department. The MRD head will now have direct access to ensure that the business processes and personnel are given topmost attention to ensure their performance, which will directly reflect on the performance of the organization.

Re-organization will require re-locating teams and team members and providing facilities. This will definitely involve costs. My advice is not to spend too much time initially, assuming that all changes are not final. During the setting phase, some typical industry or business-related aspects may require further alignment that surfaces only when we experience practical working and not evinced previously while you were simply considering the change. Permanent arrangements can be made after a few months of implementation as satisfactory results become evident.

You must also consider the fact that a few functions will be shifting to other departments. This requires a period of adjustment to the change. For example, 1) the accountants coming under MRD and working in the plant environment, 2) sales working under the MRD and working alongside technical personnel like engineering and operations or manufacturing.

It requires an open mind for the various function heads such as materials, engineering and manufacturing to work under a new coordinating director instead of reporting impersonally to the CEO. It must be understood that the position of these heads in no way signifies demotion because they are not reporting to the CEO directly as they were doing earlier or compared to those who head the marketing, finance and HRD functions. These positions remain at par for the tangible or intangible function heads. The MRD head's position is in between the CEO and the functional heads and as such becomes the second-in-charge of the organization. The responsibilities between the CEO and the MRD head become segregated if you consider the MRD department activities in general as a day-to-day activity going by the nature of the tangible activities such as daily manufacturing, ordering/re-ordering, dispatches, etc.

The activities of the intangible departments such as finance (having shifted materials accounting to MRD department), marketing and HRD are not a daily activity in the strict understanding of the term. They take day-to-day actions that mature or yield results over a period of time. For example: marketing pursues a customer for an order which may take days, weeks or months, or HRD arranges recruitment or arranges a three-day training which may require activity to be done months before the actual training takes place.

The CEO is also not a day-to-day function. Besides monitoring daily labor, as mentioned earlier in this book, this position requires action directed toward the perpetuity of the organization. Therefore, besides reviewing day-to-day activities the CEO's maximum focus will be on long term sustainment and growth activities. This requires the CEO's close working with marketing, finance and HRD. With the MRD, the CEO will now be able to review at one point all manufacturing and engineering activities and work on implementing long term plans.

When the re-organizing work is done, the next step is to define the responsibilities of the various tangible and intangible functions of the business.

STEP 5 - WORKING THE MRD WAY:

Having set up the organization as per the MRD concept, now we need to define the responsibilities of all the business functions under MRD, the tangible activities as well as the intangible activities- marketing, finance and HRD. For this, you can follow the general responsibilities mentioned in Chapters 3 and 5. You can tune the responsibilities as required for your typical business set-up. The essence is that the responsibilities must ensure that the three major fundamental principles of the MRD concept are achieved by focusing on materials. This includes conservation of natural resources, avoiding pollution and protecting environment, and improving the business process for more efficiency and effectivity.

You must train your MRD professionals to become 'Techcomphi' professionals so that you will develop the 'all-rounders' who can work in any business function within the MRD department. This will be a great asset for the MRD head, as I mentioned earlier.

STEP 6 – INTEGRATING SRM AND CRM:

After establishing the internal working of the organization the MRD way, the next step is to integrate the organization's suppliers and the customers into the organization's business process as extended arms on either side. As mentioned in Chapter 6, the first step is to understand the organization's standing in the market. This is very important as any effort to bring the supplier or the customer closer will not work till such time as you are able to build trust with them. This means that you must work at the basics of the relationship and remove the irritants in the relationship such as delayed payments, delayed deliveries, or poor quality for the customers.

Once you start working earnestly on various issues concerning the relationships, the suppliers and customers will increase their trust in you and will then start working toward your organizational goals. Under MRD this becomes easier because all the concerned business processes will work together and, with better SRM and CRM being their common responsibility and goal, will not only resolve the supplier and customer issues but also find permanent solutions as compared to the earlier organizational set-up.

Besides this, understanding the type of business situation you are in will enable you to use the right approach and techniques to build up the relationship. The aim is to work toward a 'Perfect 10'on SRM and CRM. As you work toward this, the 'Profitability Continuum' starts delivering its results!

STEP 7 - THE MRD REVIEW:

The MRD department must review its work on a weekly and monthly basis. The aim is to assess the 'Before MRD' and 'After MRD' performance and take corrective actions as required to ensure the fundamentals of the MRD concept. This must go on for at least a year until the new system stabilizes. Thereafter, the review can be on a monthly basis.

MRD must set up their own business parameters to measure their efficiency. Essentially it should reflect performance in three main areas, which is the essence of the MRD concept i.e. conserve materials and energy, stop/avoid pollution and improve efficiency in the business process, all of which will lead to saving costs and increasing profits.

Below are some points for evaluation, as examples that can be considered in terms of material waste and pollution. These are:

1) Material losses, damages in transit of in-coming materials/outgoing materials.
2) Material losses, damages, wastage within the organization.
3) Material wastage re-used/sold for reuse/sold to recycling companies/ scrap dealers/ sent to waste disposal plant.
4) Materials lost in usage due to negligence or poor technology (chemicals evaporating, etc.)
5) Materials saved through value engineering or value analysis activities(reducing obesity)
6) Materials saved through use of new technology
7) Materials saved through new design
8) Energy in any form which saved – reduced consumption
9) Alternate form of energy used – wind/solar
10) Reduction in pollution because of new technology
11) Reduction in pollution owing to better maintenance
12) Reduction in pollution owing to improved processes
13) Pollution stopped
14) Plant, machinery and equipment maintenance cost down
15) Emission reduction in logistics/ transportation
16) Above, part of vendor and customer awareness and training
17) Achievement sharing on above with the business fraternity

BUSINESS RELATED:

18) Lead time reduction in various business processes within and end-to-end
19) Cost reduction in the final product (Reducing MS Ratio)
20) SRM and CRM scores
21) Inventory reduction

EMPLOYEE RELATED:

22) Improvement in employee morale
23) Achieving objectives and goals

The above are a few points that stress material conservation, re-use, recycling, energy saving, pollution reduction and business performance improvement in terms of lead time and cost reduction. You can add any business parameters pertaining to the MRD activities and responsibilities and monitor the same. A good management of the MRD activities will guarantee results.

THE MRD MODEL:

Based on the Seven steps toward implementation of the MRD concept in your organization, we will now see schematically how the MRD model will look like.

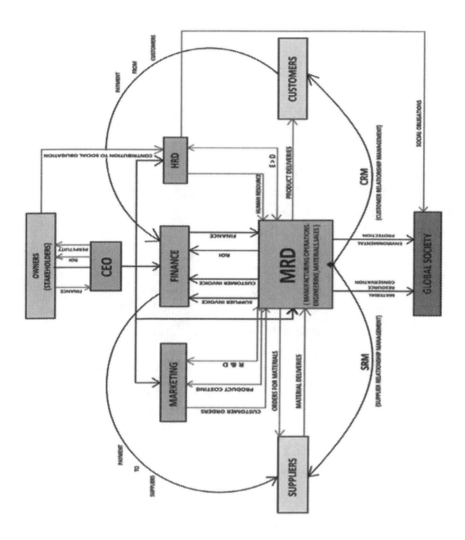

THE MRD MODEL

Let me explain the MRD model to you.

At the top, we have the Owners of the organization who are the stake holders who invest and arrange the Financial requirements for running the organization. They expect profit in return. After all, Business thrives on profit!

Besides providing finance and running the organization thru a CEO who handles the day to day operations of the organization, the Owners, under the MRD concept, are also expected to contribute some part of their profit, whatever be the amount, toward social obligations. This will include environment protection activities, social upliftment like hunger and poverty alleviation and the like. The Owners and the CEO must get this done through HRD.

The CEO, as the leader of the organization, runs the day to day activities through the functions of Marketing, Finance, MRD and HRD reporting to him or her. The CEO runs the organization with the finance from the Owners and is expected to give the Owners ROI ie Profits. The CEO's other major responsibility is to ensure growth of the organization and its perpetuity both of which take care of the longevity of the organization.

We will now look at the four functions reporting to the CEO.

Besides all the major responsibilities we saw in the earlier chapters for all the departments, the MRD model shows the major aspects in the MRD activities in a MRD organization.

Therefore, in the MRD model, Marketing will receive the product costing from MRD for all its customer enquiries to enable them price the product and marketing will pass on the customer orders to MRD for manufacture and delivery. They work together on R&D activities.

The Finance department will provide MRD with Finance and MRD is expected to give a good ROI. Finance will receive money from the Customers based on invoices raised by MRD for all the dispatches made to the customers and Finance will pay to Suppliers based on the supplier invoices approved by MRD.

HRD will provide MRD with human resources and both will work together for maintaining and increasing E>D (efficient/deficient employees intelligence). HR is also a spokesperson for the organization and the responsibility of publicity and image building is also their responsibility. A new role HRD will play for the Owners directly is the contribution to the society towards various social work, based on the allotted funds by the Owners. They will also combine with MRD to share with the industry or business world their experience and innovations in materials conservation and environment protection.

MRD, besides their responsibilities mentioned in the earlier chapters, activities mentioned above will interact with its 'right and left hand' ie the suppliers and customers, in ordering and receiving material from suppliers and delivery of quality product to the customers and maintaining the supplier and customer relationships and enhancing the 'profitability continuum'. Their responsibility towards the global society, irrespective of country borders, will be to ensure natural resource conservation and environment protection in the activities they are involved in as well any other contribution possible.

A STORY:

Now, let me sum it up with a story!

There was a very hard working brilliant professional in the materials management department in an organization. He had started his career with this organization as a purchase assistant.

He had two strong points: one was that, at the start of his career, he did all his work-related management studies while actually working. He graduated in materials management, international trade and business management by attending evening college for five years. This gave him a sound business management base that helped him perform well directly in his work related to procurement, international business- imports and exports, warehousing and logistics management.

Second, he put into practice, simultaneously, what he learned at the business college, which gave him practical experience of the theories learned and gave him positive results at work.

Over the years, with this business knowledge, he could look at the materials management function for the entirety of the organization. This helped him cross the barriers of departmentalization and work at serving his internal customers (a new Japanese philosophy in those days) in production, marketing and engineering to achieve their goals and that of the organization.

As a materials head, he saved material-related costs every year, first to make his salary free for the organization then the salary of his department. After this, the savings were to ensure a lesser materials to sales ratio which was a regular contribution, year after year, to the profits of the organization.

He had put in long years of service and over the years, by sheer performance, rose from a purchase assistant to a materials management position.

One day the CEO of the organization called him and gave him both happy and sad news! The good news was that he was being promoted to a divisional manager's post!

However, the sad news was that he was being transferred to take charge of a loss making unit of the group. He took it as a de-motional promotion! He was upset, wondering whether he'd be able to turn around the loss making unit. If not, he could lose his job and that would affect his career. He thought about his wife, twin daughters, and the housing loan!

He was upset, as he was not sure whether he should accept the new assignment or not. So he decided to seek advice from his *Guru,* an Indian word assigned to a person whom one regards for his philosophical and spiritual knowledge.

The *Guru* listened to him patiently and when he had finished relating his problem and concerns, the Guru excused himself, walked out of the room and came back in a few minutes carrying a pocket size packet in his hand.

The Guru asked him to take up the new assignment and, handing over the small packet, told him, "Keep this with you. When you go to your new workplace, every day in the morning, take a round of all the areas in your plant with this in your pocket."

The Guru gave him two conditions, one, that he would never open the packet and, two, to return the packet after exactly one year. The professional, considering the packet as some kind of a magic wand, gladly took it. Then, thanking the *Guru,* he left, promising not to open the packet and to return it after one year.

The professional took up his new assignment and did exactly as he was told by his *Guru.*

Every day, first thing in the morning, he would tour the entire plant with the packet in his pocket. It appeared that the packet or the magic wand, as he considered it, started yielding results! The correctives and improvements he started making at the loss-making unit, started giving him results. He managed to bring the unit to a break-even point by the first half of the year and by the end of the year, he was showing profit. He had turned around the unit!

He was very happy. But one thought made him sad: the thought of returning the packet to his Guru. He hated to return the magic wand that had brought him success. But a promise is promise, he said to himself, and went to meet his Guru.

After telling his success story, he profusely thanked his *Guru* and, very sadly, parted with the packet. He wished to know what was in the packet and longed to have the packet for one more year, by which time he would be able to establish his unit firmly. But he could not gather the courage to ask his Guru for the packet for one more year.

Thanking his *Guru* again, with a heavy heart he started to leave. The Guru sensed the professional's dilemma, called him back and making him sit said, "I know you would like to know what is there in this packet and you would like to keep this with you for one more year." The professional, with all humility, said, "Yes, *Guruji,* please let me keep the packet for one more year." His eyes filled up with tears of gratitude, for the Guru himself offered what he longed for.

The *Guru* then proceeded to open the packet. When the packet was opened, the professional was shocked by what he saw. The professional had expected some gem stone that brings luck in the packet but what he saw was an ordinary stone!

The *Guru* smiled and asked the professional, "What did you do with this stone?" The professional then told the Guru how every morning with the packet in his pocket, as told by the Guru, he went around his plant and met all his employees. They were very pleased to see him visit them every day, talk to them, enquire about them, and show interest in their family and work.

Over a period of time the employees became friendly with him and started sharing their work-related problems. Then, the first step he took was to set right all such work related problems and make changes in systems, procedures and processes that enabled the employees to perform their work better. He created a sense of value for all types of material resources within the unit among the employees.

He then encouraged the employees to give ideas and suggestions for improvement in their respective areas, implemented the ideas, and rewarded those whose ideas were implemented. After that, he visited and invited the suppliers and customers to air their problems, so he could correct them and receive any suggestions for improvement. These were implemented. All this, of course, improved the productivity, morale and performance of the employees and improved the supplier and customer relationship, ensuring smooth flow of supplies from the suppliers and more orders from the customers. All this put the unit back into a profit-making mode!

The professional's face then suddenly lit up. He said, "O *Guruji,* now I understand why you told me to take a round everyday of the plant. It was not to take the stone to every area of the unit but to take myself to every area of the plant! And this has made the entire difference!"

The Guru smiled.

Thanking the Guru profusely, the professional left, fully confident of his abilities and with the lesson that business cannot be handled by sitting in your chair. You must be in touch on a daily basis with two invaluable resources, that is, your human resources and the other - your MATERIAL RESOURCES!

The logic behind the MRD concept is: In business, focus on what is worth focusing on, control what is worth controlling. In this context, material resources are worth both your focus and your control.

Every organization, whatever its size, can contribute to material conservation and environmental protection.

A journey of a thousand miles begins with a single step

And

Every drop eventually makes an ocean.

However small a business unit may be in service, trading, or manufacture, every business unit must take the first step toward conservation of our natural resources and protecting the environment. We have come a long way in our depletion of our natural resources and degradation of our environment. It's a long way ahead to rectify it. But the first step must be taken and any contribution, however small, must be made. MRD is one effort in this direction.

It is very important that we create awareness at a macro-level, the national and global level. However, success will come only when it is implemented at the micro-level, every industry level, every business sector and any level of business. This must become a part of our business culture.

In business, we must think about every idea that can make us do our business with our community in mind and also make profit. The MRD concept helps you achieve both. **After all, Business thrives on Profit!**

Author: Natarajan Satishkumar

N. Satish kumar is a Certified Supply Management Professional from NLP, USA and a Postgraduate in Business Administration with specialization in Materials Management. He holds Diplomas in Business Management, Materials Management & International trade .He has a Bachelor's degree in Commerce.

He has more than 25 years experience in the Materials and Supply Management field and has worked as Materials Manager and Purchasing Manager in various industries in India and the Gulf such as Electrical & Engineering, Electronics, Chemicals, Service, Food, Plastics & Paper industry. This experience gives him a wide-angle view of the Materials Management and Supply Management applications in various industries. He also lectures on Materials Management subjects.

He has various articles related to Supply Management published in Supply Chain & Logistics magazines and has also presented in Supply Chain Management Conferences in Dubai and Singapore on Supplier Relationship Management.

Visit web site:
www.mgmtexcel.com
Contact author at:
satishkumar1102@gmail.com